FOUNDATION OF IT OPERATIONS MANAGEMENT

Event Monitoring and Controls

MR. PRAFULL VERMA and
MR. KALYAN KUMAR

ACKNOWLEDGEMENTS

Acknowledgements from the author

I am very happy to bring out my second book. I conceived the idea to write this book when I was halfway through my first book. I also started work on it before completing the first book, and at some point, both were being authored in parallel.

As with my first book, my thanks go to all who helped me to bring out this book: to all those who provided support, talked things over, read, wrote, offered comments and remarks, and assisted in the editing.

I would like to offer a note of special thanks to a few individuals in particular. To begin with, I want to thank C. Vijayakumar, whose continued support and input made this production easier. C. Vijayakumar's original vision of cross-functional service as a discipline in IT service management and his support for me in this area will remain the foundation of all my work and creativity. Among my colleagues, I would like to thank Vineet Gangwar, whose point of view was thought provoking for me.

I want to thank my wife, Annie, who motivated me to work simultaneously on the second book and shared the typing load to overcome my fatigue. At the time of our marriage, she accepted me as an engineer, and now she has accepted me as an author, and I am happy with this new image.

I also want to thank my daughter, Naomi, who demonstrated a great deal of patience during my work and gladly accepted my nonparticipation in some of the important home activities.

Acknowledgements from the coauthor

Once again I would like to acknowledge the support of my better half, Zulfia, who provided me the space and freedom to focus on this endeavor, and also on my musical journey, by carving out some family time. I would like to acknowledge the important teaching from my four-year-old son, Azlan, who keeps teaching me that "the Child is father of the Man."

This book is dedicated to people engaged in managing IT operations and keeping the business alive

TABLE OF CONTENTS

1 FOREWORD

O ver the past 50 years, we have seen tremen-
dous changes in technology, from traditional
systems, networks and storage in the datacenter, to
new systems of engagement including mobile, social,
cloud, and the internet of things. While these technologies are reinventing IT infrastructure and services across industries, the proven fundamentals and
best practices of event management and monitoring
remain constant.

Given these external forces, the role of information technology has become a
strategic business driver and competitive advantage, when done right. Today's
business leaders have higher expectations on how IT can help them quickly
take advantage of emerging opportunities. To provide this level of value to
the enterprise, organizations need the ability to flawlessly deliver and manage
IT services and processes, all while factoring in internal and external dependencies. The combination of these forces has created a strong need for event
management as a key enabler of a powerful and efficient IT infrastructure.

This book focuses on advancing the process of event management as a strategic point of control for IT operations, and as a means of assuring service

1

quality and continuity, irrespective of the mix of vendor technologies, or tools in use by an organization. It is intended to be an educational tool for the IT generalist, and also provides new insights for seasoned IT leaders. Upon reading this book, any IT professional should have a foundational understanding of the complex technical process of event management.

Deepak Advani

GM - Cloud & Smarter Infrastructure
IBM Software

2 PREFACE

In our earlier book, *Process Excellence for IT Operations: A Practical Guide for IT Service Process Management* (http://tinyurl.com/k7u3wyf), we discussed the significance of process-driven IT operations. In continuation of the same theme, this book focuses on process excellence of the event management process, more commonly known as the event monitoring and control process in IT operations. In the context of IT service management, you can also call it service monitoring and control. This is applicable to the operation of contemporary IT infrastructure that includes corporation-owned and -managed data centers and clouds. Event monitoring and control for cloud-based computing is included in the scope of this book.

The purpose of this book is to extend the message of the first book—that process excellence matters—with the sole focus on one specific process that we believe is the single most important process in IT operations: the monitoring and control process. Although this is not an IT infrastructure–specific process, we see it in practice in all the aspects of business, government, and life. You want to monitor everything that concerns you and your business. Depending upon the criticality of the thing or the conditions or circumstances, you decide what you will monitor and to what extent you will do so. For example, you monitor your own health, and we suppose a routine health check at regular intervals is the minimum ritual you believe in. This may turn into real-time monitoring for a patient who is in ICU. Retailers monitor their active stocks of merchandise for sale and take proactive actions for stock replenishment to do better business. Airlines continuously monitor their flights in real time to manage their services. Similarly IT operation managers monitor the IT landscape to keep an eye on the operations and to ensure that IT can continue to perform.

The secondary purpose of this book is to demystify the tool-dominated operation management of IT infrastructure and clarify that it is the automated process at the core that produces the result, even though the process activities are not visible like in other processes. In fact, this book is inspired by the one of the famous statement of Dr. W. Edwards Deming "If you can't describe what you are doing as a process, then you don't know what you're doing."

William Edwards Deming was an American statistician, professor, author, lecturer, and consultant who promoted the "Plan-Do-Check-Act" methodology. It was popularized by ITIL as the Deming Cycle, although it was not conceived by Deming but by Dr. Walter Shewhart. Although Deming's work was not in IT industry at all but ITIL emphasized its applicability in service management. Later in Deming's career, he modified PDCA to "Plan, Do, Study, Act" (PDSA) because he felt that "check" emphasized inspection over analysis. He did not believe in relying on quality inspection but emphasized improving product quality in development, design and production.

In IT Operations we know that tools are doing lot many things for us especially in event monitoring they do all the event processing. Yet the most of people do not know what is going on as a process and choose to rely on the result of the process. This book emphasized on the process perspective of event management, which is hitherto untouched by any other publication. Ironically Deming considered the approach of relying on technology to solve problems as an obstacle for bringing in quality by process. This book will provide an additional paradigm to operation people.

The audiences of this book are people who have direct stakes in IT operations and/or some interest in understanding this area. It is not necessary to be a tool expert or technology expert to grasp the majority of the contents of this book. We have chosen to minimize the technical aspects of event monitoring and controls, as there is enough guidance from tool vendors in the context of their tool implementation. While vendors can definitely provide the tool implementation guidance, the process implementation guidance is not in their area of focus. This book addresses that gap in which event monitoring is not treated as process implementation. Hopefully this will be a useful attempt to fill in the gap. At the same time, this book will present both aspects of event management to IT professionals: how simple are the concepts and how complex is the implementation.

3 INTRODUCTION

IT has become an integral part of almost all businesses and enterprises. Even not-for-profit organizations, governments, and social programs have IT at the core. IT provides an execution platform for a business's strategy and operations that allows a business to win market share, delight customers and stakeholders, increase efficiencies of operations, and more.

Today IT is the lifeline for almost every business and industry. Airlines, banking, manufacturing, health care, and all other service industries rely on uninterrupted operations of computers, networks, and applications.

In order to keep your business running, you must keep IT services running and keep them healthy and protected. There are multiple levels of monitoring to achieve these goals:

1. You monitor to ensure that all the components of the infrastructure, from the lowest level (hardware) to the highest level (applications), are working as expected.

2. You monitor to ensure that the services or the outcomes for the business, such as the transaction or the end-user experience, are being realized.

3. You monitor the security threats and risks to keep the services protected and secured.

The principle underlying all the above levels of monitoring is the **event management process**, which detects events at all levels, processes the events, and carries out the actions on the events. The event management process is thus the foundation of all service management processes. Almost all of the monitoring is continuous through a variety of tools, and this maturity level has come a long way in past two decades. Most often these elements are popularly known as *availability monitoring* and *performance monitoring*, although the core of the process is the events that are impacting availability or the performance of the component or the service. In the earlier book, we discussed service quality gaps and how processes can close those gaps. Historically the quality of service (QoS) has been the key criterion in all service contracts, and it includes requirements for all aspects of a connection, such as service response time, loss, signal-to-noise ratio, crosstalk, echo, interruptions, frequency response, and loudness levels. Now customers are also talking about quality of experience (QoE) in IT services. Event management is the primary enabler for monitoring the QoE parameters, such as transaction time or the overall end-user experience.

How proactive monitoring evolved

Monitoring was in place since the first generation of computers, when mechanical and electromechanical components formed the significant part of computers. After the generation of card-punching machines, which were largely mechanical, came the era of magnetic-tape drives, line printers, drum printers, Winchester drives, and so on, which used electrometrical components that required regular checkups. Prafull has himself followed the practice of the preventive maintenance in old systems—checking mechanical parts, lubrication, and wear-and-tear inspection, pretty much like a car inspection during maintenance. Power supply and signal level checking were also part of this preventive maintenance.

The evolution of monitoring tools kept pace with advancements in computer technology, and real-time health monitoring of the mainframe became an integral part of the mainframe system itself. As early as 1991, Digital Equipment Corporation built the VAX 9000, which had a MicroVAX II–equivalent system built in and dedicated to its own health monitoring.

As software engineering advanced, software-based dedicated monitors were developed by independent and third-party vendors and created a separate market segment. These monitoring products were technology specific and had limited functionality. Today the market is highly mature, with a wide choice of monitoring tools having advanced functionality that matches with real business needs.

Monitoring tools versus event management process

This book does not intend to discuss monitoring tools but intends to focus instead on the event management process that is enabled by the monitoring tool. One important point must be remembered: monitoring tools do not provide the full functionality of the event management process, nor do they fully automate the complete event management process, as might be claimed by the tool vendors. It is the event management process that brings effectiveness to the monitoring and control for any service.

Event management process in ITIL

Many people believe that the event management process was introduced in ITIL V3, but that is not true. It came into prominence in ITIL V3 because it was placed in the *Service Operation* phase along with incident management and problem management. However, it was very well covered in ITIL V2 in the *ICT Infrastructure Management* book. For most people, the ITIL V2 world is confined to two books—namely, *Service Delivery* and *Service Support*. The depth of ITIL V2 was far beyond these two books, and in fact the depth of guidance on the event management process in ITIL V2 is more than that in ITIL V3.

Practical guidance in this book

This book covers two complementary aspects of the event management process: the functional viewpoint and the technical viewpoint. For a complete and effective design and implementation of the event management process, you need both aspects, though in real life, we have witnessed that event management process implementation is largely deemed the tool implementation. In fact in the earlier book, we mentioned that even ITSM process implementation is deemed the tool implementation, and we emphasized the need for a functional consultant in ITSM implementation. The same equation applies here as well. When both are combined, you know how the process should work as a whole and how the tool can enable it.

4 BASIC CONCEPTS AND DEFINITIONS

Hierarchy of event, incident, and problem

An **event** is an action or occurrence within the system in scope that has some significance on the operations. It is manifested by a change of state that has significance for the management of a configuration item or IT service. With every event, a message or a piece of data is associated that provides information about one or more system resources. Therefore, the term *event* is also used to mean a message or a notification created by any IT service, configuration item, or monitoring tool. Events typically require IT operations personnel to take actions and often lead to incidents being logged.

Event can also be defined as the observable situations or modifications within an environment that occur over a time interval. An event may be a state change or reporting of an activity by a single component within a system, or may be an interaction between multiple systems. Events may occur at differing levels of abstraction and at multiple places along the log management path. As such, an event can describe an original (base) event, an aggregated event, or a correlated event.

An **event record** is a collection of event fields that together describe a single event. Terms synonymous with *event record* include *audit record* and *log entry* Throughout this book *event* is also used as shorthand for *event record*.

A **log** is a collection of event records. Terms such as *data log, activity log, audit log, audit trail, log file,* and *event log* are often used to mean the same thing as *log*

An **alert/alarm/warning** is an unqualified or qualified message from a monitoring tool that indicates that some error condition has occurred and requires attention. An *open alert* does not imply that the service is impacted. In this book the terms *alarm, alert,* and *warning* are used interchangeably.

An **incident** is an event of interruption or disruption in service. Incident implies that service is impacted.

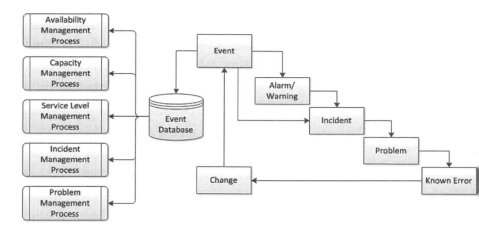

Figure 1: Event Incident and Problem Hierarchy

A **problem** is an unknown, underlying cause of one or more incidents. This could be the occurrence of the same incident many times, or even events or diagnostics in events and incidents revealing that some systems are not operating in the expected way. A problem can exist without having immediate impact on the users, whereas incidents are usually more visible and the impact on the user is more immediate.

A **known error** is an incident or a problem for which the root cause is known and for which a temporary work-around or a permanent alternative has been identified.

Figure 1 illustrates the hierarchy of event, incident, and problem.

Importance in IT services

IT systems, components, and services derived from those systems and components usually do not deteriorate abruptly, but they definitely deteriorate gradually. The rate of decay is dependent upon a range of factors, such as what something is made of, how it is used, and the environment in which it is operated. Regardless, the degradation below the usable level can be detected ahead of time. Event detection and monitoring is thus the crucial early warning system for IT operations and service management. The root of all incidents and problems lies in some event that may or may not have been detected. The maturity of the event management process will bring in the visible change in the operation and shift the paradigm of operation from crisis management to planned actions.

Event management and service monitoring

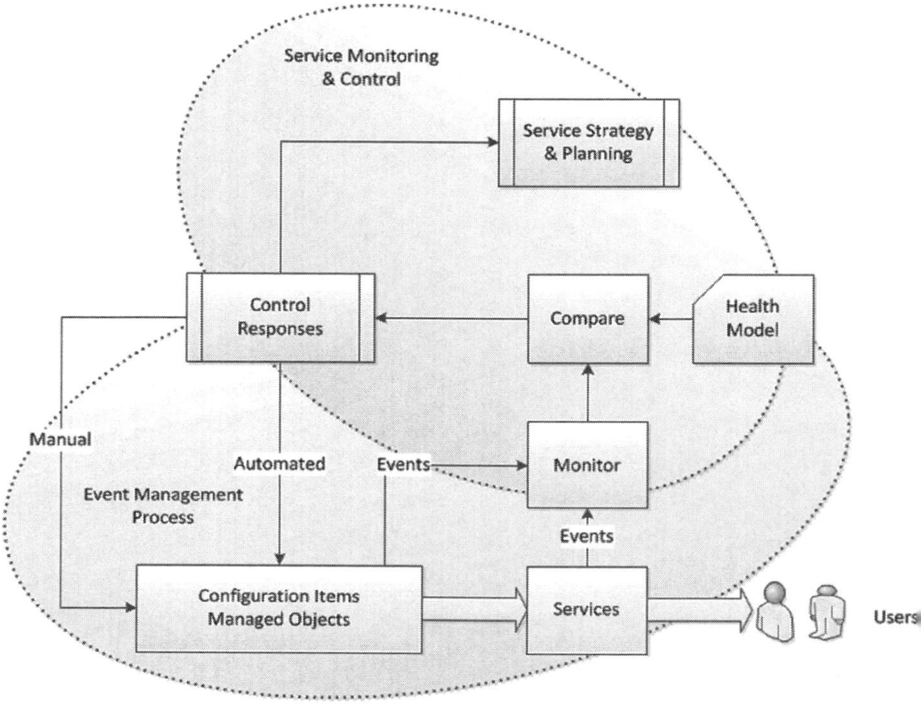

Figure 2: Event Management vs Service Monitoring and Control

Event management and service monitoring are very closely related but are slightly different in nature. **Event management** is focused on detecting meaningful events, processing those events, and identifying the events that have negative impact or potential negative impact on the service, and then acting to prevent the negative impact. It is a matter of **event lifecycle management**.

Service monitoring focuses on the monitoring beyond events—for example, analyzing the usage patterns and related data for use in service strategy and planning. Capacity management is a very good example of service monitoring.

Configuration item versus asset versus managed object

A **configuration item** (CI) is a component of the infrastructure that produces or contributes to the production of IT service. A CI is a component of IT infrastructure that needs to be managed because it has an impact on IT service. CMDB is a complex database, but configuration management is a relatively simple process.

An **asset** is an item that has economic value. An asset database is relatively simple, but the asset management process is complex, as it has a much longer lifecycle.

In the previous book, we discussed the difference between an asset and a CI. Asset monitoring and/or CI monitoring are often referred to as event management, but that is not the right terminology. We actually monitor the managed objects that may or may not be a CI.

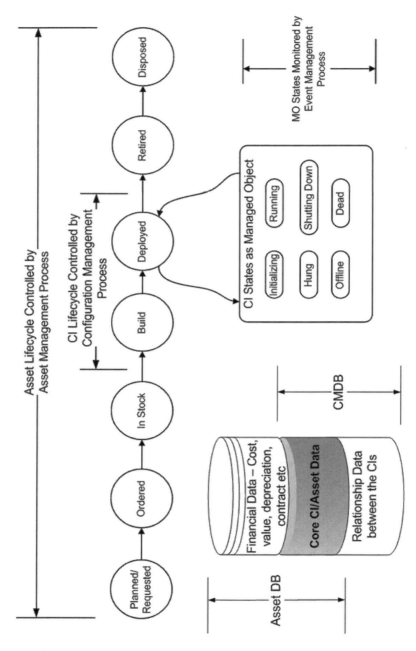

Figure 3: CI vs Asset vs Managed Object

A **managed object** (MO) represents the operational properties of a CI that are related to the operational behavior. It is the management view of the system resource that is subject to operational control. The event management process is the cornerstone of this operational control.

In operations, managed objects are dynamic in nature. For example, if the Exchange Server is up but the RPC service is hung, e-mail service will be unavailable. Here the Exchange Server as CI has little relevance on event monitoring, but RPC service as the managed object is far more relevant.

For the sake of simplicity, you may consider the monitored parameter as the managed object, and for that purpose, some of the MOs can even be static in nature—for example, memory in the server—but remember, we monitor memory utilization, not the absolute memory.

Instrumentation is the mechanism that is used to expose the state of the managed object in a CI. Generally instrumentation is well built for the CIs below the application layer, but in both packaged and custom applications, it is not properly built; therefore it is often a burden on process. The good news is that the event management product vendors have come forward to fill in the gap in this area, and they provide a variety of probes.

Service maps

A **service map** is a graphical representation of a service that illustrates how the service is built using various components. These components generally include hardware, software, and their relationships. All of the data to build and show the service maps is stored in the CMDB. Many people want to add configurable settings or roles, as well as customers and other services, to the service map, but that kind of system would be too complicated to build. The purpose of a service map is to gain an understanding of the service's structure to manage it. A service map is not the only thing that is required to manage the service, and the roles, configuration setting and other attributes. are required as well to determine how the service is delivered and controlled, thereby ensuring expected availability, capacity, security, and manageability.

Service maps bring in a lot of value in documenting an environment because they

- present a service-centered view of the environment;

- create a bridge between technology and business by organizing technical capability in business-oriented terms;

- facilitate understanding of complex systems and component dependencies.

However, service maps should not be seen as the substitute of end-to-end information at the micro level. The following table explains what a service map is and what it is not:

Service map is	Service map is not
Abstracted information of the structure of a service that is derived from multiple sources, including service design documents such as an architecture overview	A replacement for service design documents, such as an architecture diagram
A map for navigation to determine the impact of a component on the service	Recorded in a service portfolio or service catalogue

Service maps serve the event processing by providing data for correlation and impact analysis of events. Service maps today are implemented with various differences across the tools platform, which leads to major chaos in reconciling and identifying authoritative sources. Service maps are the core artifacts not only to help manage the business service but also for the service integration in a multiservice provider environment. Service Integration and Management

(SIAM) is gaining momentum in the ITSM world, and it will be a subject of another book that we intend to bring out in the near future.

There are three methods through which tool vendors can build service maps today:

1. Use CMDB discovery to create service maps and then import it them from the CMDB in an event management tool—this approach will become irrelevant in a dynamic IT landscape as discovery tools are scheduled and not real time.

2. Use the application transaction model to discover service dependencies—this approach is apps down but leaves out the details of the infrastructure elements.

3. Use the native discovered data by element managers and create service maps at the event management tool—this approach ensures that authoritative sources feed the service maps. The key point to manage is that the integration of data models from different tools can lead to complexity.

Service catalogue, CMDB, and service maps

A **service catalogue** is the published list of all services in production. A record in a service catalogue will include the key service attributes. CMDB is the database of all configuration items. A CI record will show the key attributes of a CI. A service map will use the CMDB and service portfolio data to illustrate the structure of the service and its relationships with different CIs.

Event management as the foundation

In Figure 1 we can directly deduce that event is the foundation of incident, problem, and changes. There are a few fundamental solutions that truly glorify the event management process, and these are the industry-favorite buzzwords used by research companies and tool vendors. We take this opportunity to discuss two of such hot buzzwords—namely **business service management** (BSM) and **application performance management (APM)**.

Vendors use BSM in their marketing messages and always relate it to the strengths of their own products. BSM is not just a product; it is a methodology that is enabled by multiple products and, more importantly, a set of service management processes.

A true BSM system will enable a set with the following functionality:

- Understand the enabling business service by IT.

- Map it to the underlying configuration items within IT infrastructure.

- Maintain the maps that are dynamically changing (possibly real time; but all tools do not support real-time map maintenance).

- Monitor and manage end-to-end service by monitoring and maintaining the state and performance of CIs using an appropriate set of processes and tools.

BSM is a layer above IT service management, and the IT service management must be mature enough to support BSM.

Similarly, APM is about monitoring the applications-related managed objects such as the application processes and transactions, linking them to business service through service maps, determining the business value, and then delivering rapid, proactive problem identification and triage to help resolve problems before they impact end users and critical services.

The selling point of application performance management is that it allows IT organizations to be in control of customer experience by enabling them to proactively identify, diagnose, and resolve problems before end users and revenue-generating services are affected, while assuring consistently high service levels that meet the demands of business.

In other words, both buzzwords mean a comprehensive combination of event management process plus CMDB plus service maps in action.

Security monitoring and event management

Security monitoring is actually an event monitoring and control process with a specialized purpose. Here you monitor and control (detect, defend, recover) the events that are characterized as security events, such as unauthorized access to the services and/or the systems and components that are producing the service. A typical example is log-file monitoring to detect potential threats. Successive log-on failures for a privileged access is one prime example that is considered a possible attempt to gain unauthorized access.

5 EVENT LIFECYCLE MANAGEMENT VERSUS EVENT PROCESSING

5.1 Rule before Tool

Event lifecycle management (*event management process*) is a *service management process* that deals with the full lifecycle of event while *event processing* (refer process event box in figure 4) in one of the subprocesses within event management process. The event management process will have all the components of the process such as rules, roles, policies, guideline, input, output, RACI, measurements, and reporting. Tools perform the *event processing* tasks within the event management process in an automatic manner and may not have all of the independent components mentioned above.

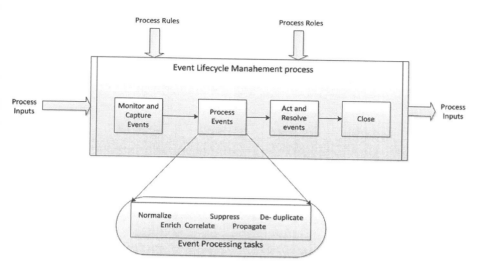

Figure 4: Event Management Process Model

The detailed discussion in the next section will clarify this concept.

5.2 Event Management as a Process

The following seven diagrams—Figure 4 through Figure 10—provide the process perspective of a typical event management process. The purpose of these diagrams is to present the end-to-end view of a mature event management process. All the diagrams are self-explanatory. It is important to note that tasks shown in the diagrams may be executed by an individual person or by a tool or by scripts/programs. It is possible to automate almost everything, and we can eliminate the manual part of the process completely. Some of the events that arise out of defects and cannot be automatically diagnosed and fixed are in fact the incidents and problems.

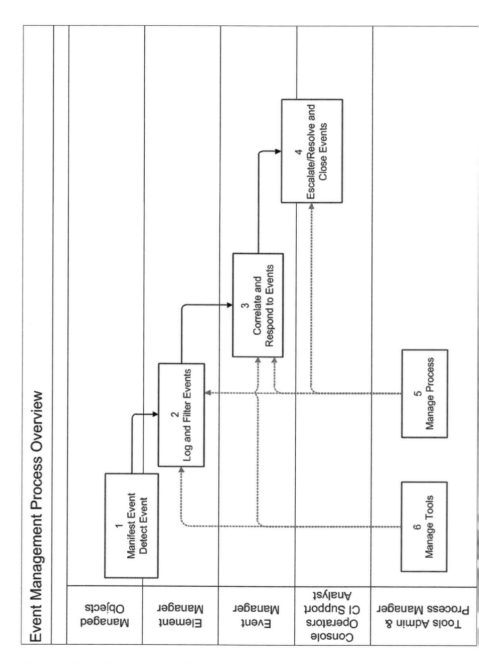

Figure 5: Event Management Process: Overview

As shown in Figure 5, the event management process defines six subprocesses and seven roles. Most people do not consider subprocesses five and six as part of the event management process, but we strongly believe that managing the process *and* managing tools must be institutionalized in all organizations as an integral part of the event management process.

As you see, machines are playing the major roles in the process. Roles that are mapped to humans are console operator, CI support analyst, tool administrator, and process manager. People who need to understand the details of process management should go through our earlier publication, *Process Excellence for IT Operations.*

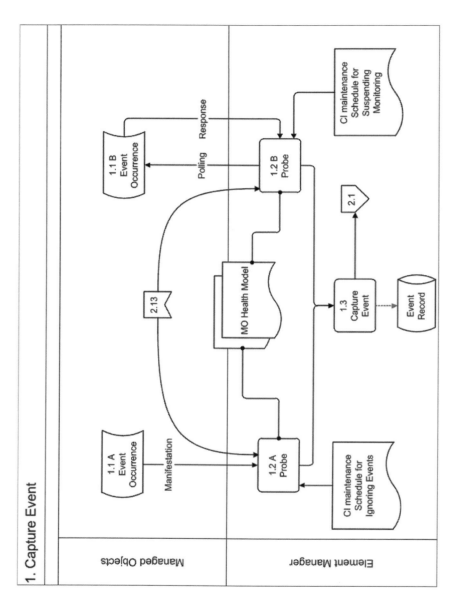

Figure 6: Event Management Subprocess 1 of 6

A managed object can manifest an event without polling, but sometimes polling is required to capture the events.

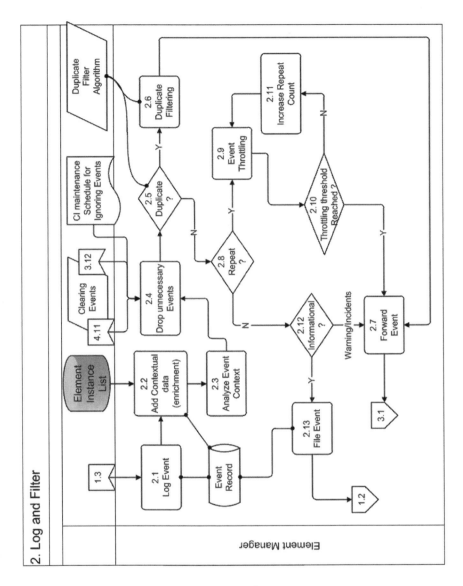

Figure 7: Event Management Subprocess 2 of 6

Filtering is a series of specific specialized steps. These are suppressing, throttling, deduplication, etc. The quality and relevance of contextual data added before the filtering are extremely important for efficient and effective filtering.

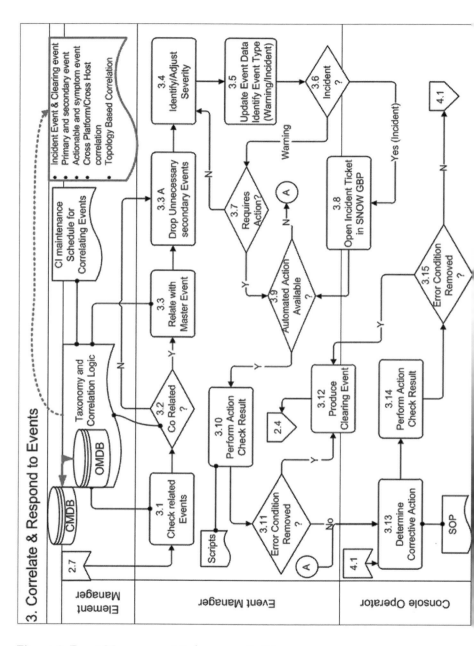

Figure 8: Event Management Subprocess 3 of 6

Correlation is the association of two or more log entries of unique events. Correlation can be used to group events into a series, often by time sequence or causality. Correlation is extremely complex and has multiple facets. One aspect of correlation is relating the events from different CI sources based on the relationships of those CI. Another facet is relating the events from the same source based on the sequence of operation. (Fault event and clearing event are the technical terms used for such correlation.)

Another approach to correlation is to analyze patterns based on algorithms and also human knowledge input to identify causal discrete patterns, which can lead to events being generated.

Responding to an event could be manual or automated action.

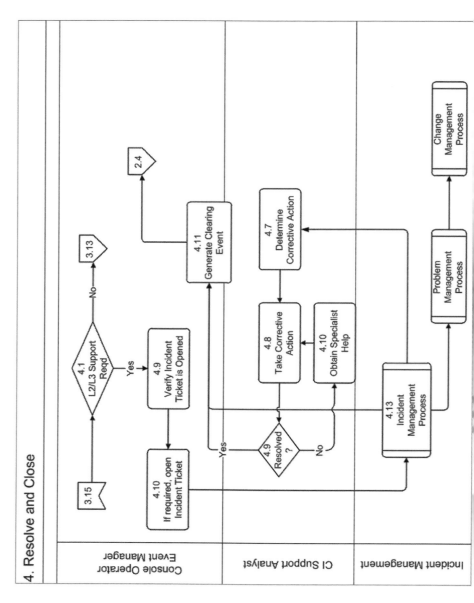

Figure 9: Event Management Subprocess 4 of 6

Whether it is a warning or an incident, the event must be followed through to its logical end state.

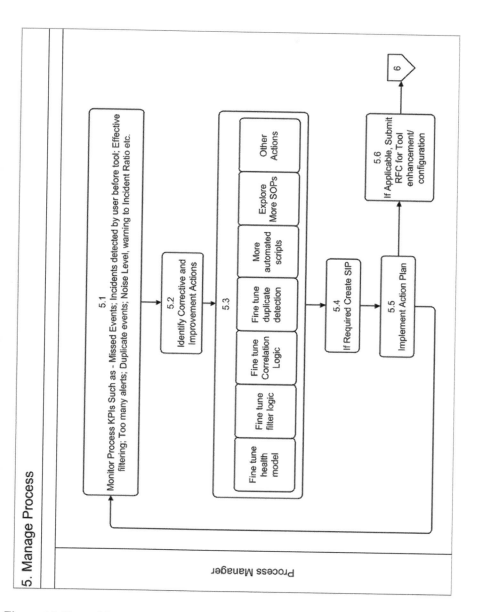

Figure 10: Event Management Subprocess 5 of 6

This is the pictorial representation of what process management means for the event management process.

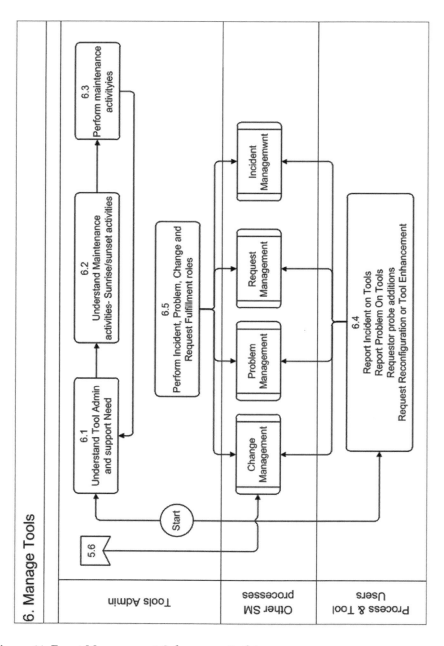

Figure 11: Event Management Subprocess 6 of 6

All organizations have tool admin and support in place, and not much explanation is needed to justify the need of tool administration and support. However, it should be institutionalized and governed by the service management process itself.

5.3 Generally Observed Deficiencies

In most of the implementations that we have seen in the industry, we have witnessed a few common gaps:

1. The part of the event management process that can be done by the tool configurations is implemented, but the rest of the parts are ignored. That means the event processing is implemented, not the full event lifecycle management process

2. Subprocess 5 is ignored almost everywhere. The process is not managed. There might be some ad hoc reconfigurations, but once the "tool" is implemented, everything is deemed as completed, and ongoing improvements as depicted in the diagram are missing.

3. Subprocess 6 is very ad hoc and not well governed.

As a consequence, the process loses its efficiency and effectiveness, and that is reflected in the IT operations in terms of inconsistent workloads.

In a later section on operation support, we discuss in detail how to address the deficiency of subprocesses 5 and 6.

5.4 Completeness of Process

Let us understand what the typical inputs and outputs of an event management process are, and then we will automatically be able to map which one lie beyond the event processing tasks. You can determine the completeness of the event management process in your organization by assessing whether the process in your organization is producing these outputs or not. If not, you may find that some inputs are missing and/or the process is not adequately designed.

Outputs of the event management process	Inputs required for the event management process
Incidents, warnings, and information	Control response scripts and SOPs
Control responses to events	System events
Events transaction records	System/MO health model
Updated SOPs	Monitoring requirements
Knowledgebase on event behaviors	Maintenance schedule
Event instrumentation	Infrastructure details (CI List, CMDB)
Template for tool configuration data	Filtering and correlation rules
Reports	SLA
Updated health model	SOPs
Updated monitoring requirement	

5.4.1 Outputs from the Process

Incidents, warnings, and information

The event could simply be information, or it could be an alert or an incident. Informational events are not processed for any action but are filed for other purposes. Examples of informational events are a successful log-on or log-off, a batch job completion, and a completion of a transaction. Certain kinds of data collections also happen through this kind of event—for example, resource utilization data that does not warrant any action but will be provided to the capacity management process for analysis.

Warnings or alerts do warrant some action. These are still not incidents but have the potential to become incidents if not acted upon in a timely manner. "File system is 80 percent full," for example, is a warning that has no impact on the service. However, if you do not act in time and make free space available before it becomes 100 percent full, the application will stop running, and this would be classified as an incident.

Some events are incidents and need higher-priority attention. "A device is down or not reachable," for example, is an incident that has an impact on the service and needs resolution on priority.

Control responses to events

The event management process is expected to define/establish the control response for the different classes of events. The control response could be automated or manually executed. The control responses are usually established in the form of standard operating procedures (SOPs) and/or scripts or orchestrated workflows for automation. The number of predefined SOPs and the level of automation determine the efficiency and effectiveness of an event management process.

Events transaction records

Every event has a finite lifecycle, and that is recorded as the transaction. The event management process creates and maintains the database of each transaction. There are multiple uses for this database, and it is the source of a variety of reports—for example, availability reports and performance reports.

Updated SOPs

Standard operating procedures are the inputs for the process, but the process is responsible for keeping the SOPs current. Thus the updated SOPs are the output of the process.

Knowledgebase on event behaviors

In any IT infrastructure, the system's behaviors depend upon the way it is being used. Similar systems can produce different kinds of events depending upon the method of use. Similarly different kinds of events cause different kinds of impact in the environment and may further produce related events. A good process will create and maintain the knowledge base for symptoms and causes, and in fact this will be the source of creating and maintaining the SOPs.

Event instrumentation

Instrumentation defines how a system will expose itself or the managed objects for the purpose of monitoring. Windows Management Instrumentation (WMI) is the Microsoft application of the Web-Based Enterprise Management initiative for an industry standard for accessing management information. Likewise SNMP is a defined standard for network devices. Across the industry there has not been much development to standardize instrumentation protocols and metrics across the IT landscape leading to proprietary implementations. Most application vendors design adequate instrumentation for monitoring their applications; however, you may land up in developing one, if it is not available for your application. The event management process maintains and uses the instrumentation information to capture the events.

Template for tool-configuration data

Instrumentation knowledge further leads to the creation and maintenance of the templates that are used to deploy and configure the variety of tools.

Reports

Reports are the fundamental outcome of any process, and the event management process is no exception. The process creates and maintains the event management database, and that is the source of a variety of reports. It is important to note that the monitoring tools are not reporting tools, but these tools must be capable of capturing the required data to produce the desired report. A process implementation will include the reporting requirements and, based on these requirements, will define the data points to be captured.

Updated health model

Health models are the input to the process, but they continue changing as the ways in which systems are used keep changing. The event management process must update the health model, and thus the updated health model becomes the output of the event management process.

Updated monitoring requirement

You do not monitor anything and everything. What to monitor is driven by the business needs and SLA, and just as the business is dynamic and keeps changing, monitoring requirements get modified. The event management process maintains the updated monitoring requirements. This includes the addition of the managed object and CI list under the scope of the process.

5.4.2 Inputs for the Process

Control response scripts and SOPs

Every alert/warning or incident requires a definitive response. The best practice is to pass on the incident to the incident management system, where it can be managed by the incident management process and brought to closure. Alerts should be responded to with scripts or SOPs.

System events

System events are the beginning point or the trigger of the process. This is the most fundamental input to the event management process.

System health model

The health model defines what are deemed healthy conditions (operating within normal conditions) or unhealthy conditions (exception) and the transitions in and out of such states. The right information on a system's health is required to compare the current condition and determine health deterioration. The health model seeks to determine what kinds of information should be provided and how the system or the administrator should capture the right events to assess the deviation. Some parameters can be normal for one system but may not be normal for a similar system being used in a different manner. For example, the 75 percent CPU utilization of a transaction server could be normal, but 25 percent CPU utilization of a file server could be considered an overload.

Monitoring requirements

The question of what events to capture for what purpose defines the monitoring requirements and is driven by the business. The correct form of this input to the process would be the managed object list with the deviation tolerance.

Maintenance schedule

You would suspend the monitoring or ignore/discard the warning events originating from a configuration item and managed objects within it if you are performing scheduled maintenance activities. Process uses this schedule as input data to determine when to suspend the monitoring.

Infrastructure details (CI List, CMDB)

The infrastructure details represent the list of the managed objects under the scope of the event management process. The change management or release management processes would update this list. When you modify the infrastructure or release some new services, the change or release are the primary control to trigger updates in this list.

Filtering and correlation rules

Filtering and correlation make the event management process effective and efficient. The rules to do so are based on the service maps (and therefore the data from CMDB) and the logic of preventing as well as suppressing undesirable events for processing purposes.

SLA (service-level agreements)

Service-level agreements (SLAs) really shape the actions on potential outages or service breaches that are detected by events. The process needs to know the optimal time to act and resolve the issues. SLAs also influence the monitoring requirements, although the monitoring requirement itself is one of the inputs to the process.

SOPs (standard operating procedures)

SOPs do provide prescribed activities or tasks. These can be executed automatically or by a person and form the first-level control response to the events demanding action. SOPs determine the efficiency and effectiveness of the process and form important inputs to the process.

5.5   Event Processing

After detecting an event, a series of actions must be performed on the event before a conclusive response can be initiated. What this series of actions will be depends upon the kind of event and the origin of the event. Here is a summary of these processing actions:

1. Capture: Receive the raw and unstructured data from the source element and hold it in the memory temporarily; data is captured via two methods: (1) self-manifestation and (2) polling by the probe and capturing the response.

2. Normalize: Convert unstructured data into structured data so that the processing logic can be applied in definitive field values.

3. Discard: We do not want to process the event further if we know at this stage that it does not make any sense to do so.

4. Throttle: If a source is generating an alert storm, then suppress all events and create a new event indicating that an alert is generating an alert storm. An alert storm can be defined by configurations—if a source has generated more than five alerts per second.

5. Deduplicate: Deduplication is the process of collapsing the duplicate events into the original event. The original event will indicate how many times and when duplicate events occurred.

6. Blackout: Identify maintenance windows from the declared maintenance schedule and handle the events during this period differently. Monitoring tool should stop notifications and ticket generation if a CI is under a maintenance window.

7. Correlate: Associate two or more log entries of unique events. Correlation is used to group events into a series, often by time sequence or causality.

8. Enrich: Enrich events with additional data, as from CMDB or other sources such as flat files or databases.

9. Trigger Autoaction: Actions to be taken by tools when alerts of certain criteria are received, such as emails or pings.

10. Assign: Automated method of resolution may not be available and a person should take the manual action; the purpose is to assign events to operators.

11. Propagate: The event is now propagated to the next level in the hierarchy, most often as an incident into another system outside the event processing system, for further actions.

The next section elaborates these processing stages.

5.6 Explanation of Process Stages

5.6.1 Capture

The objective at this stage of the process is to generate meaningful information on the health of the managed objects that is of significance to the effective operation of IT services. Various event detection mechanisms may be used These include the following:

- SNMP traps

- Log file

- Polling through agentless mechanism

- Polling through agent-based systems

- Streaming feeds from agent-based systems

- Adapters for collecting events and data from element management systems

SNMP traps

SNMP traps enable an agent to notify occurrence of significant events through an unsolicited SNMP message. The idea behind trap-directed notification is that if a manager is responsible for a large number of devices, and each device has a large number of objects, it is impractical for the manager to poll or request information from every object on every device. The solution is for each agent on the managed device to notify the manager without solicitation. Agent does this by sending a message known as a trap of the event.

Traps are generated when a condition has been met on the SNMP agent. These conditions are applied to the data defined in the management information base (MIB) provided by the vendor. The device administrator defines thresholds, or qualifications to the conditions, that should generate a trap, and a packet is sent to the SNMP trap host, or manager. Trap-directed notification can result in substantial savings of network and agent resources by eliminating the need for overwhelming SNMP requests. However, it is not possible to totally eliminate SNMP polling. SNMP requests are required for discovery and topology changes. In addition, a managed device agent cannot send a trap if the device has had a catastrophic outage.

Traps are network packets that contain data relating to a component of the system sending the trap. The data may be statistical in nature or even status related. SNMP traps are alerts generated by agents on a managed device. These traps generate five types of data:

1. Coldstart or warmstart: The agent reinitializes its configuration tables.

2. Linkup or linkdown: A network interface card (NIC) on the agent either fails or reinitializes.

3. Authentication fails: An SNMP agent gets a request from an unrecognized community name.

4. egpNeighborloss: Agent cannot communicate with its EGP (exterior gateway protocol) peer.

5. Enterprise specific: Vendor-specific error conditions and error codes enabled by the device vendors.

All network devices work on SNMP. Microsoft provides an SNMP agent, or client, for Windows. By default, Microsoft SNMP agents do not trap anything under enterprise specific. This can change, however, depending on what is installed on the host.

Log file

Log files are everywhere in all systems. A log file is a file that contains a list of events that have been "logged" by a computer. An operating-system-maintained log file is the most important object for the monitoring and control in IT oper ations. Syslog Standard is the general standard for a logging system, which allows the filtering and recording of log messages. Additional objects of inter est for event monitoring are the following:

- OS log file
- Database log file
- Application log file
- Webserver log
- Clickstream log

These log files are important sources of information. Unfortunately, this is no fully structured data, and it may also be a challenge for all members of the staf to be able to interpret all types of messages in all types of logs.

Log-file monitoring probes are available for almost all popular monitoring products, and they monitor targets and multiple kinds of objects such as log files, web pages, messages from queues, and outputs from commands.

Probes capture the events of interest for further event processing. Some probe also do the partial processing; for example, they can automatically inform about error situations immediately after they have occurred.

Probes can be configured to monitor ASCII log files in any format. All log files do not have the same layout. Some files are line oriented (single-line files like the UNIX system log files /usr/adm/messages), while other log files are record oriented (multiple-line files, like the ones produced by Oracle). The probe moni tors line-oriented and record-oriented log files just as effectively using a power ful regular expression and/or pattern-matching scheme. The probe checks the log file for new entries at user-configurable, timed intervals, keeping track of the position within the file between each run. This assures that only one alarm is sent per log entry, even if the log file is truncated in the meantime.

A probe can be configured to monitor many log files. Within each log file, it can be set up to look for occurrences of many different log-file entries. Different log-file entries can trigger different alarm messages, which may contain text from the log file and/or user-defined text set up by the person who configured the probe.

A probe runs through a set of profiles that essentially contain information about the monitored objects—that is, the file to monitor, how to monitor it, what to look for, and how to react to the event.

Response to probe

Managed objects are constantly polled to collect event data. On the detection of a valid event, a response is sent to the probe, where it is crosschecked against maintenance schedules to ensure that the event is not to be ignored or suppressed. On validation that the event is a legitimate and meaningful occurrence of failure or threshold breach, an event record is captured in the central event-management tool.

The event record should contain the following information:

- Event ID

- Event status

- Event processing state

- Relationship

- Symbolic name

- Category

- Type (availability, performance, security, informational)

- Level

- Message description

- Probable cause

- Activity log

- Source file

Agent-based and agentless polling

Historically, network monitoring has been agentless monitoring using SNMP-based polling of network devices from a central management station, while application and server monitoring have been agent-based monitoring performed by software agents locally installed on the servers. As operating systems and applications have evolved, enhanced monitoring capabilities have been built into these infrastructure components. Using these built-in monitoring capabilities, we can now monitor servers and applications in an IT infrastructure in an "agentless" manner. With this approach, remote server monitoring is possible where a central data collector will remotely connect to a server and monitor the availability, performance, and usage of a server and the applications that it hosts.

Yet the depth of the diagnostic information obtainable from the agentless approach is limited. The agent-based approach provides deeper, broader monitoring because the piece of software (agent) sitting on a local system can deliver deep and wide information. This information makes event processing more effective and efficient—for example, correlation and control response are significantly enhanced with the help of the enriched information that an agent can deliver.

Adapter-based collection

The adapter-based approach is to connect to an underlying element management system that is monitoring the end managed object. The adapter-based approach collects the events generated by the element manager and converts them into the event record format for event processing. The adapter may also collect all the underlying instrumented data and feed it into an analytics engine for intelligent processing.

Streaming feeds from agents

With modern IT environments and in the case of large volume and velocity of data, streams processing is another new mechanism being used in event management. This approach uses a big-data-based architecture, which allows for very large volume and speed of event streaming data being sent for event processing. The scenarios of streaming feeds are applicable for the public cloud, Internet-of-things sensors, cybersecurity feeds, etc.

5.6.2 Normalize

When you are capturing data, does the event message explain clearly what the problem is? And does it offer sufficient and meaningful data to figure out a solution? In all cases the raw data has content but needs work to make it meaningful, and this process is called **normalization**. Normalization also deals with the conversion of unstructured data into structured data to make it fit for further processing. The structure makes it possible to easily apply the processing logic on events.

There are two schools of thought in normalization emerging from the structured processing versus unstructured processing (a.k.a. big data) approaches. Event management from a control action perspective would need to have a structured normalization approach, which would have to capture the relevant data to drive actions. The unstructured processing approach is to use analytics and pattern detection to drive control actions. This is an implementation-specific consideration, which needs to be taken into account. In our section on Ops Architecture, we have clearly defined the layers of applying both the thoughts- structured and unstructured processing.

Another example is the collection of data for performance versus capacity. Performance data is summarized and normalized with a time window for trending purposes. Capacity-based collection would like to retain the entire raw data set to perform more granular processing and slices. This again is an implementation consideration. The technology available today allows for both approaches, unlike a few years back, when large data-set management added more cost and complexity.

After normalization, events go through the series of filtering processes.

5.6.3 Discard/Suppress/File

This is the broad-level filtering of the events, like applying a coarse filter. Not all events are meaningful or worth analyzing. There will be much noise, and this is the first step of filtering as soon as the event record is normalized.

Discard or suppress means to get rid of the event at this stage and prevent it from entering into further processing. Events deemed to be noise are simply thrown out of the event management system.

Some events are still of informational interest and are filed for record keeping, even though they are not required to enter into further processing steps. These are used for audit purpose. ITIL calls these **informational events**, and the examples are successful log-on or batch job completion. Some of the events seem to be just informational events, such as clearing of an error condition, but this is more than the informational event because it is used to correlate with the original error condition event in the event processing system.

Event processing logic should be very discretionary to determine which events should be just thrown out and which should be filed for record keeping.

One common case depicting the value of suppression is event storm suppression. Once a message storm is detected—for example, one hundred events from an object in five minutes—a high-priority event is created indicating the message storm. Newly incoming messages will optionally be suppressed. Automatic and/or operator-initiated action is usually set at the probe or agent level.

5.6.4 Throttle

Events that fit into the qualification criteria of actionable events must be forwarded to ensure that they are responded to with an appropriate control response. However, sometimes the event source generates the desired message more than once when an incident occurs. Usually, only one event is adequate for processing and deriving the action. Also, it may not be reasonable to create a message when a threshold is exceeded only for a short time. **Throttling** is the process of reporting events after a certain number of occurrences. For example, a high-CPU condition at a certain stage in the backup process for a minute is not a warning, but if the high CPU utilization is reported several times within a specified duration, then the system would send a warning.

Throttling is thus a filtering based on the duplicate detection process that determines which events are identical and can be referred as duplicate. The time frame in which a sampling is done may vary depending upon the nature of the event being reported. Often, it should be addressed immediately when the first indication of an event occurs. This is especially true in situations where a device or process is down. Subsequent events can then be discarded. At other times, a warning/incident does not need to be investigated until it occurs several times. In this case, the event should be addressed after the necessary number of occurrences.

5.6.5 Deduplicate

Duplicate detection and suppression can be done in several ways. Depending on the managed object and predefined logic, different methods can be used.

Deduplication and throttling are closely connected and are often considered the same thing in the filtering steps.

Deduplication combines similar events identified by message key or other attributes. A counter indicates the number of duplicates. Individual events are attached as annotations and/or available in the event history. Only a single consolidated message is forwarded instead of several hundred repeated events that add noise and seek the attention of the operator. This approach is typically used with events that state a failure in a system or equipment. Immediately reporting the event minimizes the mean time to repair.

5.6.6 Blackout

All systems require maintenance, and when maintenance activities are performed on a system, they will appear as failure or erratic behavior to the event monitoring system. Most maintenance activities—such as applying a fix, upgrading software, and reconfiguring system components—are all well planned and scheduled.

During the scheduled maintenance period, the monitoring is suspended for the objects within the CI under maintenance so it will stop generating events. But there will be related components upstream in the service chain that will still be monitored and will still send events. These may be genuine or false alerts.

Blackout refers to the method of event handling—usually suspending and suppressing—during the period of deliberate system outage. It is very difficult for an event management process to handle systems that are in maintenance mode. Often it is not practical to reconfigure the monitoring agents to temporarily ignore only the resources affected by the maintenance. Maintenance may cause a chain reaction of events generated by other devices. A server that is in maintenance mode may only affect a few machines with which it has contact during normal operations. A network device may affect large portions of the network when maintained, causing a flood of events to occur.

Shutting down monitoring completely may suppress the detection and reporting of a real problem that has nothing to do with the maintenance. Both of these approaches rely on the intervention of the administrator to stop and restart the monitoring. This requires a high degree of discipline in IT operation because unscheduled and unplanned maintenance will be very difficult to manage from the event management perspective.

5.6.7 Correlate

Correlation is the association between two or more events based on some common logic or data. One aspect of correlation is relating the events from different CI sources based on the relationships of those CIs. Another facet is relating the events from the same source based on the sequence of operation (fault event and clearing event, for example).

Correlation is the most complex part of the event management process, and the maturity of the event management process in an enterprise environment is determined by how well the correlation logic is implemented. Correlation depends largely on the "knowledge" of the environment, and that comes from the CMDB and the service maps. For that reason, implementing good correlation logics in an event management system is very complex and requires significant engineering of the systems. However, some basic correlations can still be simple to implement.

When multiple events are generated because of the same error condition, correlation defines the relationship among these events and determines the appropriate action. Events can be correlated at the agent/probe level as well as at the centralized/server level. The following table compares the two methods. These are not mutually exclusive and can be used together; that is, some kind of correlation can be done at the server level and some at the agent level.

Correlation at the element-manager layer (Agent based)	Correlation at the central level (Server based)
• Decentralized: distributed processing and split of processing load • Close to the source: earlier correlation in the event lifecycle is more efficient • Independent of server and network connection	• Single point of maintenance • Can be implemented across heterogeneous environments such as composite applications or cross-domain correlation for agentless event sources • Combines events from different systems

Aggregation is the implied stage in event processing for correlation. Aggregation is the identification and combination of two or more similar log entries. Aggregation is used to identify and remove duplicate log entries or to merge the details from log entries regarding the same event instance.

Correlation of the same error conditions

The same error conditions may be detected by two different methods and will generate two different events from different sources, but both are telling us exactly the same thing:

1. Probe 1 monitors the RPC Service and detects that the RPC service died—incident event generated

2. The dying service writes an error message into the system log

3. Probe 2 reads the system log and extracts the message indicating that the RPC service died—incident event generated

The event at step one and the event at step three are related. Both are indicating exactly the same thing: RPC service is dead, and therefore the application will stop working. For corrective action, only one event needs to be pursued, and the action on one is also the action on the other.

Status-based correlation

Events are not only generated when an error condition occurs but also when the error conditions are cleared. A cleared error event seems like the informational event that just needs to be filed, but it is imperative to use this event to close the original error condition event. The warning/incident event and cleared event may be generated from the same source detected by the same probe, or by different sources detected by two different probes. This is basically the status change of the same event. The premise is that for each failure event, there should also be a way to determine when the failure has stopped or has been fixed.

Example: Error condition occurs and "error condition cleared" event—one probe:

1.   RPC service hung—error condition detected—incident event generated

2.   Automated script run and service restarted

3.   Issue resolved—"error condition cleared" event generated

The event at step one and the event at step three are related. The event in the third step will set the status of the event in the first step to "resolved."

Example: Error condition occurs and "error condition cleared" event—two probes:

1.   Probe 1 monitors the RPC Service and detects that the RPC service died—incident event generated

2.   Dying service writes error message into system log

3.   Probe 2 reads the system log and extracts the message indicating that the RPC service died—incident event generated

4.   Correlation logic should forward event 1 for action and should drop event 2

5.   Automated script runs and service starts

6.   As the issue is resolved, Probe 1 generates an "error condition clear" event

7.   The event is cleared from Probe 2

The events at step one and at step three are related as well as related to event at step six and step seven. These are not considered as duplicate events because they are originated from two different probes.

This scenario is different from a duplicate detection. Correlated events are from different event sources and could very well be in different formats. Duplicate events are of the same format and are usually from the same event source. I Probe 1 detects a down service, and repeatedly sends events reporting that the service is down, these events can be handled with duplicate detection.

Deteriorating condition correlation

In an ideal world, you will take an action on an actionable event as quickly as possible. But that may not be the best use of resources or may not be real istically possible. So in the real world, the health of the monitored object wil continue to deteriorate and there will be multiple events depicting a worsen ing condition. These events are related through a sequential relationship. You would want to record only one event for action and update the health condi tion attribute of the same record with subsequent events.

Example:

1. File system 80 percent full—*warning* event generated

2. File system 90 percent full—*warning* event generated

3. File system 100 percent full—*incident* event generated

All the above situations are related. In the net result, only one warning event record should be created, and its severity (impact/urgency/priority) should be updated with the subsequent events. In above example, the first two events are warnings because the application is still running. However, the third event is an incident because the application stops running. You would update the event record that will eventually become an incident rather than having two warnings and one incident record. When the action on the incident is taken, the clearing event will close that single incident status.

This process is similar to but slightly different than throttling. Let us take the deteriorating event example about CPU usage. The CPU is 60 percent, 80 percent, and 100 percent utilized. However, before we conclude that the CPU is XX percentage utilized, we wait for a duration in which the CPU utilization figure is continuing to exceed the threshold rather than making the conclusion on one spike of threshold exceed.

There is another possibility: that you end up generating three different actionable events and actually take action on only one, the last that is usually most severe. However, you will be required to correlate and close all three events.

Primary and secondary correlation

An incident may trigger another incident and corresponding events. The event triggered by the root incident is the primary event, and the event triggered by the consequential incident is the related secondary event. These are sometimes also referred to as the **problem event** and the **symptom event**. Symptom events are not true warnings, but to the system, they do appear as the warnings/incidents.

Example 1:

1. Probe 1 detects that the network interface is down—incident event created

2. Probe 2, which was monitoring an application, detects that the application is not responding or has timed out—"application down" incident event created

The root cause that the NIC is bad and is indicated by the primary or problem event. "Application down" is the secondary or symptom event. The application is not really down, but it cannot respond because of the lost net work connection.

Example 2:

1. File system 80 percent full—warning event generated
2. File system 90 percent full—second warning event generated
3. File system 100 percent full—incident event generated
4. File system I/O process dies—incident event generated

The events at steps one, two, and three are a single event with changing attri butes (percent value and severity value) and are related to the event at step four. Here the event at step three is still not the root cause. The root cause may be a looping application that is repeatedly writing the error log, making the file system quickly fill up.

Unlike other kinds of correlation, where you need to act upon a single event in primary and secondary correlation, you may be required to act upon both the primary as well as the secondary event.

Example of a secondary event requiring action where resolution of the primary event does not resolve the secondary event:

1. Database table full—Probe 1—incident event generated
2. Application hung—Probe 2—incident event generated
3. Database space created (manual resolution action)
4. "Database error condition clear" event generated (because of manual resolution action)
5. Application restart (manual resolution action)
6. "Application error condition clear" event generated

Events at step one and step two are related—primary and secondary events— but each requires action. Events in steps one and four, and in steps two and six, are state-based correlations, and the same event is updated.

Cross-platform correlation/cross-host correlation

Primary and secondary correlation could also be cross-platform or cross-host correlation if the source if events are different platforms or the host. Most of the time in operation, the same person will not have the required privileged access to resolve the issues on different platforms or hosts; therefore, even though they are related, both events will warrant actions from different resolvers.

Example 1:

1. Server 1 message-queue server hung

2. Message queue does not initialize

3. Server 2 application server cannot access message queue

4. Server 2 does not get data through queue

5. Transaction fails

Here you will get three different events for steps one, three, and five that are related, but from the action perspective, each may have to be resolved by a different person.

Example 2:

1. Primary firewall fails

2. Secondary firewall takes over

3. Secondary firewall sends failover message to monitor

4. Primary firewall cannot send failover message

Topology-based correlation

Topology-based correlation is basically the primary and secondary event correlation based on the network and application topology. This can very well be extended to the topology above the network layer based on the discovered information and relationships present in the run-time service model. Topology-based correlation utilizes service map information to analyze alerts and events, and ultimately establishes the primary and secondary relationships and determines which events need action. When extended beyond the network layer, it becomes the cross-platform and cross-host correlation. With modern toolsets some of these complexities are being addressed by using big-data techniques, provided there are well-defined taxonomies and naming conventions. Topology-based correlation now extends beyond Layer 2 and Layer 3 topologies into Layer 4 to Layer 7. This allows event management systems to cover the emerging modern IT landscapes where as-a-service models expose limited lower-level topologies.

5.6.8 Enrich

Enrichment ensures that the event message explains clearly what the problem is and, if possible, offers solution clues. Enrichment is the collecting and adding of diagnostic information to the event data. This information can be gathered automatically when the failure occurs and it is needed to debug the issue. This can help to reduce the MTTR for resolving the incidents originated from the event. It is also particularly useful in cases where the diagnostic data, such as the list of processes running during periods of high CPU usage, may disappear before a support person has time to respond to the event.

Incident verification is also a part of enrichment. Sometimes it may not be possible to filter events that are not indicative of real problems. For example, polling a device for its status may not produce an answer due to network congestion rather than the failure of the device. In this case, an incident event may be generated. Additional data collection is required to determine whether the incident is genuine or false.

5.6.9 Autoaction

In monitoring the world every day, you observe the same events, and every day you need to take the same action to respond to those events. In fact, you perform stereotyped repetitive activities just to keep the systems running. These activities may be simple or complex, but either way, they consume unnecessary amounts of "people time" at all levels. Thus in all environments, there are opportunities to automate the responses on events.

Typical examples for automated alerts are stopping or starting a service, allocating additional storage space, disabling the log-on, and purging a file or folder. This is a kind of run book automation (RBA) within the domain of event management process.

RBA is a vast area in IT operations. The scope of RBA goes beyond action and resolution of warnings and incidents, and many organizations have specialized products for RBA. Event management can leverage those products or even perform automated actions with the help of scripts.

In advanced and mature implementations, RBA triggered by the event autoaction logic can also automate not only the resolution action but also the change implementations. Autoscaling of computing resources or the addition of a virtual machine in a cloud environment are examples. Though autoscaling and virtual machine provisioning are considered as the change in the environment, they still are executed as automated actions based on event processing. You can make these kinds of changes as preapproved authorized changes and automate them. Similarly, in a content delivery network (CDN), an event can trigger automated dynamic delivery of contents based on the event-enriched data that is otherwise used as the diagnostic data.

5.6.10 Assign

Let's assume that our system has processed the event and determined that it requires some action. It has also attempted the possible automated action, but that did not resolve the event. So now the responsibility of an appropriate action must be assigned to a real person, and the further lifecycle should be tracked until its closure.

An assignment of an event is actually the assignment of the task to resolve the issue. The task can also be assigned by a simple e-mail notification. Most organizations use e-mail notifications to direct tasks to the right group, and then someone takes the action. This works well as long as there is no need to track the work and accountability. The real need to trace accountability comes when the service monitoring is outsourced. An audit trail is also sought in an insourced situation when an alert eventually becomes a critical incident. Apart from accountability tracing, the value of a formal task ticket creating and managing the lifecycle lies in the intelligence derived from the ticket data, which helps with workload analysis and service improvement.

Formal lifecycle tracking and reporting can be done within the event management system. Most of the event management tools allow assignment and status tracking that can be reported. However, from a practical operation standpoint, a better idea would be to propagate the further task processing to a formal incident management system, usually a part of the ITSM system (IT service management). The primary reason for this is the operational convenience. All the support persons who would undertake the resolution task will necessarily log into the ITSM system for their day-to-day operational responsibilities. This is the place to consolidate the entire operational pipeline.

5.6.11 Propagate

At this stage, the event processing has actually become the task processing. ITSM is the best task management system for this purpose. The event management system can propagate the task either as an "alert" or as an "incident." There is merit in differentiating between alert and incident even though alerts can be managed very well as low-priority incidents.

Once the event is propagated as the task in the outside system, it will wait for the closure confirmation. That confirmation can either come from the ITSM system, or the execution of the corrective task can generate the fault-clearing event, and that can be used to close the loop.

5.7 Event Lifecycle Status

The previous section described the event processing states. These states relate to the lower box of the figure 4 and internal to the tool. The table explains the status of events that relates to the event management process – the upper box of the figure 4.

S. No.	Status	What It Means
1	Open	An event record—that is, a warning or an incident—is open, warrants some action, and must be tracked from this point onward. This indicates that there is some work to do.
2	Assigned	The piece of work is assigned and the responsibility for work to be done is established.
3	Acknowledged	The assignees have taken ownership of the work.
4	Propagated	The work and the corresponding tracking responsibilities have been transferred to another system and process.
5	Closed	The work is completed.

5.8 Processing Stage Versus Lifecycle Status

Figure 12 explains where the automated event process or black-box processing maps into the whole event management process lifecycle. In the event management system that processes the event, the event ID that appears on the console is not generated until a much later stage in the processing. While much of the processing is done in the earlier stages, the event lifecycle status tracking is applied only after an event record is generated. This event record could denote an alert or an incident.

Event status tracking is primarily required to track the actions on the qualified events. These actions are absolutely necessary to eliminate the real and potential threats on service outages.

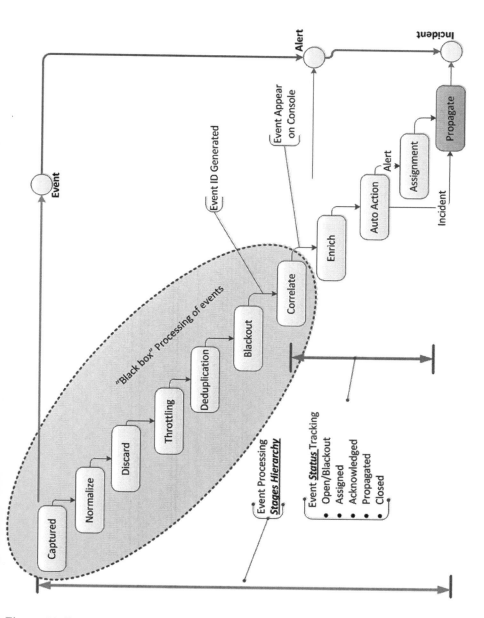

Figure 12: Event Processing Stages vs Lifecycle Status

5.8.1 Event Record

Event records may vary from tool to tool and with how the tool is implemented. The following example is a typical event record:

Field	Description
Event ID	A system-generated number
Category	Category for the event
Type	Event type as reported to the event log
Impact	Severity of event
Message description	Event message description as it appears in the log
State before	Operational state of the service before the event
State after	Operational state of the service after the event
Desired state	State in which the application or service should have been
Event group	Name of a group of related events, all signifying a transition from one health state to another
Availability	Current level of service availability in this state
Verification	Test, probe, or presence/lack of an informational event that can be used to verify whether the service is in the detected state
Diagnosis	What should be examined to determine the underlying cause of the unhealthy state reported by the event; data from events, traces, configuration settings, WMI providers, and performance counters can all be sources for diagnostic information
Recovery	How can the application recover from this state? What actions should be taken? Configuration settings, WMI providers, troubleshooters, and monitoring rules can all be used as potential recovery steps

Field	Description
Auto-retry	Does the application automatically attempt to recover from this state? If so, how often?
Clearing event	Event that indicates a possible return to a healthy state for this event; if verified, invalidates the original transition to a bad health state
Comments	General comments around this event, this state, or both
Source file	Convenience column for listing the source file from which this event is logged (note: this is optional but has proven useful for some teams doing their analysis)

5.9   Processing Stage

Although there are several processing stages, it is not necessary for every event to pass through every processing stage. Figure 13 clarifies that the number of possible transitions are a mathematical factorial of the event processing stages.

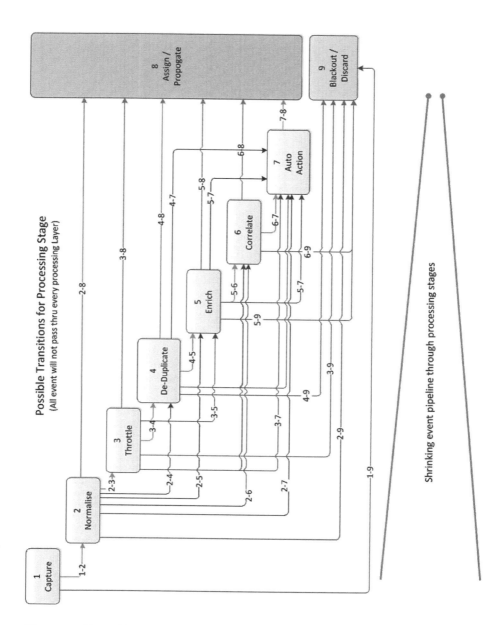

Figure 13: Event Transition through Various Processing Stages

In the event management process hierarchy, different actions are performed on the event by different processing logics and/or by different processors, as shown in Figure 13. Two important points must be noted:

1. All events will not necessarily pass through every step of processing, and they can transit from one step to another step directly, as shown by the step-connecting lines. For example:

    a. A "system down" event during the maintenance window can be directly discarded.

    b. After normalization some events can go directly through correlation or deduplication.

    c. Some events, after deduplication, can go directly to the autoaction stage.

2. The processing stages shown in Figure 13, and also referred to in Figure 12 as the black-box processing, are not necessarily in the exact hierarchy. Since the black-box processing happens within the tool, and depending upon the way you configure the tool, some kind of processing may happen in a different order. For example, the correlation can happen twice—once at the agent level immediately after normalization and again at the server level after enrichment.

Problems can arise when the event states are not consistent across the processors—for example, when an event (incident) is in a resolved state at the central event processor but not at the element processors that are in the lower tiers in the processor hierarchy. When the incident reoccurs, a new event is generated. The element processor will discard the event, and the new problem will never be reported. This kind of problem is addressed by synchronization.

Implementing event synchronization is challenging in complex environments with several tiers of event processors, particularly if the event management system is designed for high availability that requires synchronization between their primary and backup event processors.

5.9.1 Lifecycle Status Transition

While the processing stage transition corresponds to the black-box processing the lifecycle status transition is important from the service management per spective. Figure 14 provides a typical view of status transition that is intended to track the action on the actionable events to prevent the real and potentia outages on the service. This figure is for two different kinds of events: alert: and incidents.

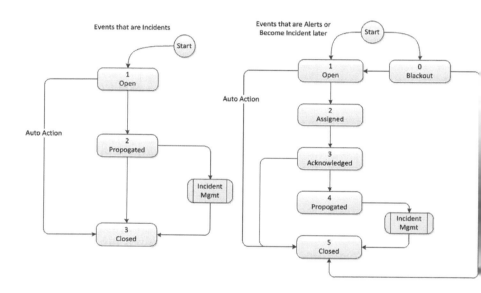

Figure 14: Event Lifecycle Status Transition

Events that are incidents

If an event is indicating a service outage, then the event management process should simply trigger the incident management process. The responsibility to resolve the incident and the ownership of the incident would be propagated to the incident management process. (We have differentiated the ticket resolution ownership and ticket lifecycle ownership in incident management process in our first book) All the actions would be tracked under the umbrella of the incident management process, and that itself would have different lifecycle statuses and corresponding SLAs. It means that assigned, WIP, and resolved statuses would actually be visible in the incident management system. The incident management process would actually close the incident and pass on the information to the event management process to make the event status closed in the event management system.

Advanced event management systems may have automated control responses to resolve some kinds of incidents, and those need not be passed on to the incident management process.

Events that are alerts/warnings

Even though an alert or warning does not indicate a service outage, it is still a potential threat to the service, and therefore appropriate action must be taken. From a service management perspective, it is important to track these actions until they reach the logical end—"closed" status. Many organizations pass on these kinds of events to the incident management system by opening a low-priority incident ticket in that system. This is perfectly appropriate, as it works very well. (This is similar to creating end-user-originated request tickets and processing those request tickets as low-priority incidents).

Most people who resolve these alerts will prefer to take the ticket assignments in a single system, which is an efficient way of working. However, we recommend differentiating between the two kinds of tickets even if both are processed in the same incident management system. One of the most important reasons to differentiate is the SLA obligation. All incident management systems are designed to measure and report the SLA for all incident tickets. If alerts are also opened as incident tickets, then service providers will be forced to undertake the obligation of SLA for alert tickets also.

5.9.2 Creating Incident Tickets

Is it really necessary to create an incident ticket? Is it not sufficient to trig ger an e-mail to the responsible person, who will deal with it and finish th required work? These are the common questions coming from the suppor groups. Answering them is a matter of service management focus. If you ar focused on managing the technology, then receiving an e-mail and fixing th problems is good enough. However, in our first publication, we indicated tha technology management is not good enough, and you need to manage the ser vice. That requires understanding the impact of this incident on service an taking appropriate actions that could go beyond the repair actions.

Let us illustrate this with a hypothetical scenario. The event monitoring detect an incident on an enterprise e-mail server indicating server outage. The noti fication is immediately triggered to the server management group. Someon sees the notification and takes the responsibility to fix it. The SLA is two hour for this critical outage, and the server is fixed within the SLA. Everyone happy Not necessarily. These actions focus on the technology, not the service. In th service management focus, you would immediately notify the service desk ir addition to fixing the server (usually through automated integration betweer the event management and incident management processes). As soon as the service desk sees the critical incident in red, it will jump into action to get read for the flood of end-user calls because of the e-mail outage. These service ori ented actions include bulletin board announcements on the portal, program ming ACD for outage announcement for all incoming calls, keeping users and customers updated, management escalations, etc. When a user calls to report the issue, he will be told by the service desk that "Yes, we are aware of this issue, and so and so is working on it, and the estimated time is xyz." All of these activities need a strong and consistent service management process.

Integration between event management and incident management is the most desirable solution, and it is very common. Although this solution is perceived as and referred to as tool integration, it is in the process integration where event manage ment process and incident management process share data on specific conditions.

5.9.3 Availability Management Support

Availability management is a specific set of interrelated IT processes and tools that need to be viewed and managed from a single vantage point in order to maintain the highest possible level of service delivery. IT processes such as change management and backup and recovery management have a direct impact on availability, while other processes such as managing configuration changes may only have an indirect impact. Following is a list of those processes and how they support the availability and event management process is the most important and places on the top of the list.

Activities Supporting Availability	Governing Process
Proactively monitor availability in real time and take actions on alarms	Event management
If availability incident occurs, resolve as quickly as possible	Incident management
Proactively identify problems and eliminate	Problem management
Control configuration changes and maintain the system up to date	Change management
Regular backups	Operational activities
Perform design audits while releasing new services	Release management
Establish availability requirements and availability SLA	SLM process
Ensure that increased consumption does not impact availability	Capacity management
Component failure impact analysis (and design audits) and risk mitigation	Availability management

One of the important responsibilities of the availability management process is to proactively monitor the availability in real time and take action on real and potential threats to the service or component availability. This responsibility is actually delivered by the event management process in ful. Availability reports are directly produced from the data coming from even monitoring.

Availability management depends on event management not only for avail ability monitoring, but also to supply the data points for the analysis, such a SLA breaches, near misses, deviations from normal operating levels, resourc contention, and over- or underusage. Although over- and underusage ar related to the capacity management data, availability is closely related t capacity. Overusage has direct impact on the availability.

Availability management uses the above data, directly coming from the even management, and undertakes the following responsibilities:

1. Establish the baseline and profiles for normal resource operation an service levels

2. Flag and analyze the exceptions

3. Predict future usage

4. Identify availability adjustment opportunities

Needless to say, the availability management process will be virtually crippled without an effective event management process.

5.9.4 Capacity Management Support

Although capacity management is a vast function in IT operations and is driven by the service capacity management, and the enablement comes from the resource capacity management, because, every service is tied to one or more IT resource. Capacity is closely related to availability. That is, if a service or resource does not have sufficient capacity, it may be considered unavailable by users. In addition, if a specific resource within a service is unavailable, the capacity of that service may be reduced.

The capacity management process starts with the collection of resource utilization data.

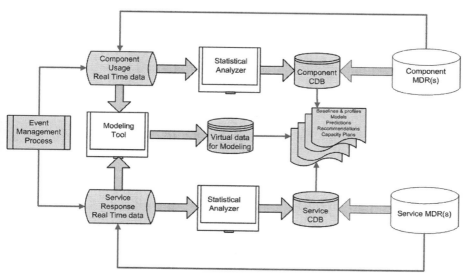

Figure 15: Event Management As the Primary Data Provider for Capacity Management

The capacity management process will

1. identify and understand the capacity and utilization of each component part of the IT infrastructure;

2. recommend optimization of hardware and software;

3. measure and store resource usage at a process level;

4. identify bottlenecks and potential future problems;

5. characterize workloads and business drivers.

Event management is the primary data provider for capacity management. There are common tools between event management and capacity management for usage data collection.

Capacity management will require additional tools for statistical data generation, analysis, and modeling. If event management is focused only on component monitoring, then only resource capacity management can be done. Resource capacity management does not guarantee that service capacity will be managed. If the event management process is designed to monitor the service, then service capacity management would be possible, but the CMS CMDB must provide a relationship between service and component; otherwise, two subprocesses will work in isolation, which will not be effective.

5.10 Tool Considerations

Every organization today possesses a wide portfolio of monitoring and control tools, accumulated over a period of time with or without any strategy. What they really need is tools portfolio optimization and a comprehensive event management process. The process part is amply covered in this book. The portfolio optimization will be discussed in the next section. Before that, we want to discuss some tool considerations that can be used for portfolio optimization and under some circumstances, such as M&A or complete outsourcing in which you may have an opportunity to build a new toolset from scratch.

As a general rule, unlike ITSM tools, where one tool can be used for multiple processes (incident, problem, change, CMDB, etc.), the event management process will require multiple tools because you will monitor multiple technologies, not just a subset. Multiple tools may or may not imply multiple vendors.

Here is an analogy with the business of travel: Every airline has an established model of hub-and-spoke service destination map, and on top of that, they have alliance and code-sharing services. Using this model they can fulfill the traveling needs of virtually every traveler. Thus for a wide-range traveler who travels to many destinations and travels frequently, the equation of convenience (or more correctly, inconvenience) among all airlines would be more or less equal, and a single airline may not have any edge. However, if the traveler is comparing for specific segments, then the equation will change. For example, if you are traveling from Raleigh to Detroit, then only Delta offers nonstop service; from Raleigh to Dallas, TX, only American Airlines offers nonstop service; and from Raleigh to Chicago, both United and American offer nonstop service. However, if you are flying between Chicago and Dallas or Chicago and Detroit, then the equations are different. Again, if you want to travel from Raleigh to Seattle, then each airline will route you through one of the hubs, and you will find all of them inconvenient. If it is an international trip to Delhi, then the airline will route you through an alliance partner or code-sharing services by another airline. Sometimes there are multiple hops, and airlines transfer passengers and baggage through well-defined processes (interfaces). You are more assured that you will not miss a connection or lose your baggage if a single airline is servicing you end to end.

Similarly, in event processing, the event will pass through multiple tools, and you need assurance about the integrity of the transaction and data within that transaction. The seamless processing is more assured if the toolset is coming from one vendor, although the tools from multiple vendors can very well achieve the seamless processing.

The tool criteria should be based on the process-enabling capability—for example, capability to enrich, deduplicate, and correlate. What kinds of data inputs are required to realize that capability? How easy or feasible is it to collect that data and maintain it? We have discussed service maps and the approaches of tools for service maps. All tools may be capable of providing correlation based on service maps, but what approach suits you?

Another important process capability is the development and maintenance of a health model. The basic concept is realized in several tools and is known as dynamic thresholds. That means tools have intelligence to understand the

health model based on the past performance of the service and set the moni
tored threshold according to the new health model.

The evaluation should be based less on the technology or method of tool to do
the job (for example, agent-based and agentless monitoring should not be key
criteria) than on the outcome the tool can deliver.

We believe that the major tool vendors in this area are equals when we consider
overall capability, as each of them has almost equal things to offer. We have
come across generic tool selection criteria by several consultants, applied their
questionnaire on all major vendors' tools, and noted that every one of them
is qualified. But the things that really matter are the implementation and the
operational architecture. Remember—a fool with a tool is still a fool. There are
primarily two types of event management tool classifications:

1. Monitoring tools, which also provide event management capabilities
   These are products that are designed to perform event management
   activities clubbed under their native monitoring capabilities. These
   systems are suited for very specific scenarios in which the monitored
   landscape is independent and isolated or a specific scope has to be
   delivered. In an enterprise-wide rollout, it is best to use only the monitoring capabilities and leave the event management subsystem to a
   top-level event manager for specialized handling.

2. Dedicated event management systems. These products are standalone
   systems that enable the event lifecycle management capabilities. These
   systems started the first evolution during the mid-1990s, when multiple
   element managers were common. Companies like Micromuse really
   evolved during this phase. During the first decade of the twenty-first
   century, the hype of having all integrated suites led to the adoption of
   monitoring/event combined systems, which led to monolithic implementations. With the second decade of the twenty-first century and adoption of modern federated/cloud-enabled services, the role of specialized

event management systems is emerging. We see emerging companies like Boundary evolving in this space, and large management software vendors like IBM and CA are developing products to support these needs.

5.10.1 Tools Portfolio Optimization

The event monitoring and control function has evolved as fragmented and silo structures in most organizations. Consequently, the tools for this purpose have been bought without any common tool strategy. It is very common to see a museum of tools with overlapping features and functionality in many organizations. Tools portfolio optimization (TPO) deals with identifying redundant tools and eliminating the duplicate functionality. It also examines the missing functionality and suggests ways to fill in gaps in the tool sets.

TPO is a strong proposition that can help an organization to improve monitoring capability and save costs. It is complimentary to the process-maturity assessment that focuses on event management as a process, identifies process gaps, and suggests improvements in the process. As stated in our previous book, taking an enterprise architecture view toward service management will lead to the adoption of an application-portfolio-driven point of view for IT management products. So applying the principles of functional-quality/technical-quality-driven portfolio rationalization is crucial to success. Event management as a process spans multiple tools' applications, and the goal should be to reduce the footprint to achieve optimal usage and effective data integration.

5.11 Tool Deployment Architecture

All tools across multiple vendors can be broken up into the following key components:

1. Probes/collectors/actors

2. Forwarders/proxies

3. Element managers

4. Integration adapter/aggregator

5. Analytics-oriented data store

6. Event manager subsystem

7. OMDB

8. Action/control response

With the current evolution in the technology landscape and the deployment of modern hybrid IT across on-premises and cloud, we recommend that, like the ITSM systems that are available to be consumed on a SaaS-based model, the core event management subsystem with the OMDB should ideally be consumed via a SaaS-based delivery model. This will allow easier integration and effective management of software upgrades in this dynamic evolution.

The deployment of probes/proxies should ideally be closer to the source of event generation, and element managers should be placed based on the network architecture considerations of where the traffic needs to be aggregated. The analytics-oriented data store should ideally be centralized or distributed based on the data volume/velocity considerations.

We also recommend a blueprint-based approach to deploy these components, which will ensure consistent enforcement of the event management process. We also recommend following the vendor-provided guidelines for the sizing of the tool infrastructure, as the product vendor would be able to provide the guidance about monitoring server loads, network bandwidth and other considerations.

5.12 Operational Architecture

By **operational architecture** we mean how the process and function will operate in the given environment. The process here implies that the tool is an integral part of it. So the operational architecture is a combination of the process, tool, function, and governance. (Governance is included in the process management function). Key components of the operational architectures are described in Figure 16.

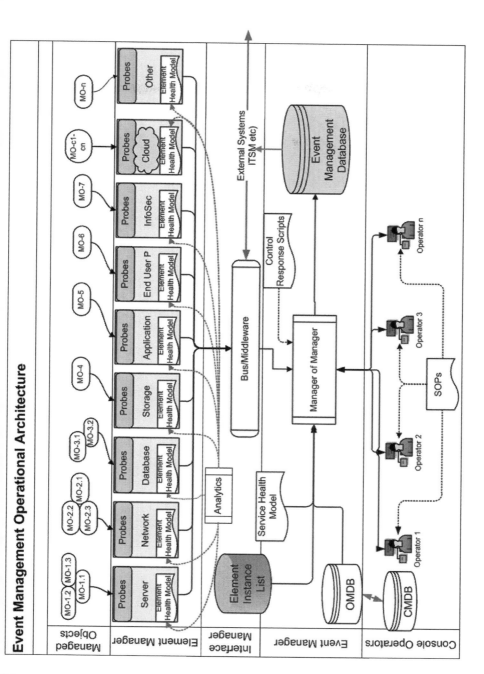

Figure 16: Event Management Operational Architecture

5.12.1 Managed Objects

Conceptually managed objects are the things of interest and therefore the tar get of the probes for capturing the events and footprints of the events. Input come from managed objects. There would be thousands of MOs that require monitoring. As you move up toward the application layer, the complexity for monitoring grows rapidly. The table below provides an example of what i typically monitored on the Windows operating system, Oracle Database, and Microsoft Exchange Server.

Operating System	Oracle Database	MS Exchange Server
1. CPU utilization 2. Memory utilization 3. Free space on all partitions 4. Server connectivity status (ping) 5. Duplicate name in network 6. RpcS service 7. Reboot	1. Check_dbalive 2. Tablespace free 3. Tablespace status 4. Index status 5. Data-file status 6. The data dictionary cache-hit ratio 7. The data buffer cache-hit ratio 8. The library cache-hit ratio 9. PGA resource consumption (monitor memory consumption of Oracle users) 10. The number of chained rows 11. User locks 12. Locked users 13. Lock waits event time 14. Tablespace size 15. Flash recovery area memory free 16. Dataguard status 17. Dataguard gap 18. System statistics 19. tnslsnr	1. Processor time 2. Database reads (attached) average latency 3. Database writes (attached) average latency 4. RPC average latency—mailbox 5. RPC average latency—client 6. Messages queued for submission—mailbox 7. Messages queued for submission—public 8. Database reads average latency 9. Database writes average latency 10. Log bytes writes per sec 11. Processor time—MS Exchange search service 12. RPC latency average—store interface 13. Hub servers in retry 14. Failed submissions per sec 15. Copy queue length 16. Replay queue length 17. RPC operations per sec 18. Application restarts 19. Request wait time 20. Average time to process a free busy request 21. RPC averaged latency—RpcClientAccess 22. Average disk seconds per read—transport 23. Average disk seconds per write—transport 24. Submission queue length 25. Retry non-Smtp delivery queue length 26. Retry remote delivery queue length 27. Largest delivery queue length 28. Poison queue length—transport 29. Log record stalls per sec—transport 30. Log threads waiting—transport length—transport 31. Reply mailbox delivery queue length—transport 32. Unreachable queue length—transport 33. Input-output log read average latency 34. Database mounted 35. Input-output log writes average latency

5.12.2 Health Model

A **health model** is the representation of characteristics and attributes that indicate that the system is in a healthy state.

To identify the different states of the application (healthy or unhealthy the characteristics indicative of these states and also indicators of the transitions between states are predefined. The health model for the basic monitoring included as part of the GBP deployment shall be provided. These may be tweaked to fit the customer environment. The product technology owner will be responsible for providing the health model for any additional custom monitoring. The model drives the development of monitoring rules, identifies health state transitions, and provides guidance on returning the application to a healthy state.

The following list provides examples of the type of information that is held in the health model for each of the managed objects:

1. What specific failure scenarios should the system monitor?

2. For each failure event, how does the system determine when the failure has been rectified?

3. Do these events relate to availability, configuration, performance, and security?

4. How are events categorized, and how is the severity matched to the impact on the CI?

5. Does the event message indicate what the issue may be, and can it offer a solution?

6. Does the service use clustering or mirroring, and how is this factored into the event detection?

5.12.3 Element Manager

In real-life scenarios, there will be thousands of managed objects with diversified characteristics across a wide variety of technologies. These are categorized according to their instrumentation and/or a monitoring technique that is usually based on the technology category. An element manager represents that category. It can also be termed as the class of a managed object. Each element can further be divided into subcategories or subclasses. In fact it is necessary to subdivide because of the great variety within a category itself. For example, all application cannot be grouped into one application element manager. From an instrumentation perspective, bespoke applications and packaged applications are radically different.

5.12.4 Analytics

Most people relate analytics to business analytics, but you should think of running IT itself as the business and apply all those principles and methodologies of business analytics.

Event management systems generate data every second of every day. This is structured and unstructured machine data and contains a categorical record of all system and database transaction behaviors, service levels, security risks, fraudulent activities, and more. While event-processing logic analyzes the data with the sole purpose of identifying and taking preemptive action for potential incidents, the analytics is a step beyond that. Analytics is the discovery of meaningful patterns in event data. These patterns are valuable in areas of capacity management, business service management (BSM), and security management. Analytics includes statistics, analysis (using complex algorithms), and operations research to quantify performance.

As you see in Figure 12, analytics is not a mandatory part from the event processing perspective but an important part to support application performance management, business service management, and so on.

5.12.5 Interface Manager

The **interface manager** acts as a gateway for data and event collection/consoli dation for internal as well as external data services. The interface managemen ideally should be treated like an ESB or message bus that supports data integra tion, data transformation, and data pipelining for consumption by internal tool and also as an integration endpoint for external systems to consume and provid data back to the event management subsystem.

5.12.6 Event Manager

The **event manager** logically is the single function that is responsible for man aging all the events. In reality, events are managed by a hierarchical manage ment function because of the diversity in the event sources and distributec event processing. At this layer in the operational architecture, it means a "man ager of managers."

In the financial and investment domain, the manager of managers (MoM concept is very common It refers to a class of financial intermediary whc hires professional investment managers to oversee aspects of a client': investment fund. More specifically, the MoM tracks the performance o: each investment manager and has the power to fire ineffective managers and then hire replacements on a client's behalf. Using a MoM to handle investment funds is an alternative to hiring a single investment portfolic manager who makes all the asset-management decisions. Because no single manager is an expert at investing in all asset classes, using a MoM allows clients to have an expert asset manager working on each aspect of an invest- ment at all times. For example, suppose that a teacher's union hires a MoM to invest its pension fund. The MoM then hires a number of investment managers, such as a bond expert, a money-market expert, and a large-cap stock expert; each has the responsibility of managing the particular asset class in which he or she specializes.

Exactly the same analogy applies here. MoM is the manager of all element managers. Each element is specialized in its own technology or service area, but each manager has no visibility outside that area. MoM has the visibility to manage across all the technology areas and has primary responsibility for correlation. MoM is the seamless technology integrator for event processing across all technology areas.

5.12.7 Console Operator

Do you really need console operators? Does this role make things better? The answers depend on the maturity of the event management process and its implementation.

Console operators are part of the command center, which is a vital function in all IT operations. The NOC (network command center) exists almost everywhere and is a narrowed version of the enterprise command center. Operations should not just focus on monitoring the network alone but monitoring the entire infrastructure and the service on top of that. This centralized monitoring and control is the enterprise command center.

The console operators will be responsible for watching the event console and taking actions on alerts and incidents based on predefined standard operating procedures. When an event is qualified as a critical incident, the command center will jump into action to manage the lifecycle of the critical incident.

In a perfect world, all the standard operating procedures could be automated, which would virtually eliminate the need for a console operator. But in the real world, that level of automation is not possible or feasible. Therefore having a console operator is imperative.

It is important that the event processing is effective and efficient so that console operators face only true warnings and incidents, and that automated control action is maximized. Apart from the key functional role in every management, the command center is also an important element of SIAM (service integration and management). SIAM is gaining popularity in the IT world, and this subject deserves a dedicated book, which we intend to bring out in the near future.

6 OPERATION SUPPORT

6.1 Process Management

In our earlier publication, *Process Excellence for IT Operations*, we explained in detail about what "process management" means and why it is required. Here are some specific responsibilities associated with this function.

General process maintenance

The process manager monitors and reviews the performance of the process by analyzing KPI reports such as missed events, percentage of incidents created by event management, effective filtering, number of unwanted/suppressed events, and warning to incident ratio. The process manager also reviews all required CIs and associated MOs and ensures that they are covered by the monitoring tools. The number and level of detail of standard operating procedures are also reviewed periodically with the view of resolving as many events as possible at the console-operators level.

The review of the process will invoke improvement tasks, which may fall into one or more of the following areas:

Maintenance of health model

The health model defined may require amendments over a period of time. This may be warranted by the changing IT environment. Additional event enrichment may also be required to make the events easier for the console operators to understand, identify, and resolve. It should be the responsibility of the technical SME/CI owner to request an amendment to the health model. This should be done via a formal process such as request fulfillment.

Fine tuning filter logic and correlation

The filtration logic may require fine-tuning to throttle or suppress duplicate events. The correlation logic may also require fine-tuning to correlate events based on defined criteria or updated network topology. These requirements can originate from any one of the process managers, SMEs, or even the console operators.

Enhancement and expansion of automated control response

The primary aim of the event management process is to detect events, make sense of them, and control their impact by resolving as many as possible at the first layer. This will be matured over a period of time by increasing the number of automated control responses.

It should be the responsibility of the technical SME/CI owner to provide automated control response scripts for known events and predetermine which managed objects these control scripts are to be executed on. These additions to the monitoring tools should be done via an approved change request and validated testing.

Enhancement and expansion of SOP

It may not be possible to automate all control responses. To ensure that as many events as possible are resolved at the console operators' layer, the standard operating procedures should be enhanced and expanded.

Create and manage SIP

Any improvements identified by the process manager or requested by the console operators/technical SMEs will be captured as specific actionable tasks and managed as a service improvement plan or as part of a larger project and released as per the agreed schedule.

6.2   Tool Admin and Support

Understanding the maintenance need

All tools need to be maintained, just like other applications. Incidents and problems will be detected on monitoring and event management tools, as will requirements for changes. Additionally, there will be requirements to perform maintenance activities to ensure that the tools continue to perform efficiently and are monitoring the required managed objects at the desired thresholds.

Any maintenance that impacts service availability should require an RFC to be approved prior to executing the maintenance tasks. All other tasks should be performed as part of the daily or weekly maintenance schedule, with no separate RFC raised. This does not include requests for additional monitor ing, updating of the health model, enhancement of event enrichment, or other change requests for new services, as these should be performed within the agreed window.

Establish maintenance schedule

Usually tool vendors provide guidance on maintenance needs and the sched ules that should be faithfully followed. Usually a weekly maintenance window is suggested, and all routine maintenance activities are performed within the agreed-upon scheduled maintenance window.

Additionally a daily activity checklist should also be performed, which shall require no RFC (example: check to see if any additional local storage disk have been added to the servers and include them in the monitoring; check agent health status; and restart the agents if required).

Resolve incident, problem, and change tasks

Tools also break down and lead to incidents, problems, and change work. The event-management-tools support staff/administrators monitor the queue of incident, problem, request, and RFC tasks assigned to this support group and resolve as per the incident, problem, service request and change process defined for service management like any other service.

7 CLOUD MONITORING

The differences between traditional computing and cloud computing are the business model and the service consumption model. It is largely a commercial model, and the infrastructure components are the same. So the fundamentals of event monitoring will remain the same, and some adjustments will be required from the business model perspective, which we will discuss here.

In the cloud, many of the elements are dynamic. For example, a VM is running, shutting down, or initializing. Within the construct of a CI, it would be impossible to manage these states. The MO view of the VM with a dynamic, changing condition will help to monitor the cloud using the same principles we apply to traditional infrastructure. Many managed objects and CIs in the cloud are also assets, as they carry a financial value directly associated with consumption and have to be metered. From the event management perspective, the question is not how to monitor the cloud (because the technology is the same, only the delivery and consumption models are changing); the important question is who monitors what in the cloud. To answer this we need to examine the service model and roles in the cloud service chain.

Service provider chain and the role

Typically the cloud service delivery chain will include the following roles:

1. Service creator

2. Service aggregator

3. Service deliverer

4. Service consumer

5. Service bill payer

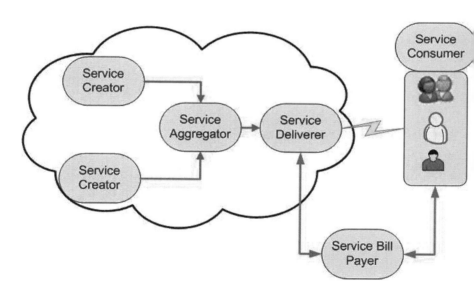

Figure 17: Simple View of Cloud Service Delivery Chain

This chain can be more complicated, as shown below, because these roles are not mutually exclusive and one actor can have multiple roles

1. Within the service aggregator role, there can be one or more service integrators (or the aggregator can also do some level of integration). To make things even more complex, the aggregator can also be the service creator for one of the service components. For example, the aggregator obtains the Iaas from the Iaas creator and the PaaS from the PaaS creator, and creates its own SaaS.

2. Within the service deliverer role, there can be the service integrator role (or the deliverer can also do some level of integration).

3. Within each role there could be the possibility of "outsourcing." For example, the service deliverer may outsource the service support.

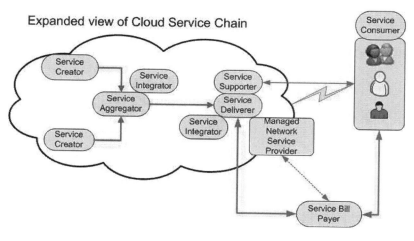

Figure 18: Expanded View of Cloud Service Delivery Chain

Now let us map these roles in the cloud service layers as given in Figure 19. There are multiple service providers in the service delivery chain; hence each provider will monitor his service layer. In the traditional IT environment, the IT organization assumes the role of service creator, service aggregator, and service deliverer, so the IT organization owns the event management for all the layers of the infrastructure.

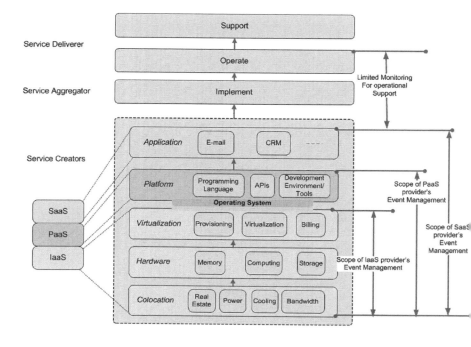

Figure 19: Cloud Service Layer Ownership in the Service Delivery Chain

In the creator role within the cloud service chain, each creator will be respon
sible for implementing and operating the event management process for hi
part of the service.

Aggregators, integrators and deliverers will be responsible for monitoring th
whole service availability but not the end-to-end event management. Mos
often aggregators, integrators, and delivers will also be the service creator for a
least one component; therefore, for all practical purposes, they will be design
ing and implementing an end-to-end event management process for thei
scope of creation.

Let us take an illustrative example. XYZ, Inc., an IT organization, is buying Iaa
from Amazon to build its own business application and deliver correspond
ing IT services. XYZ, Inc. is also buying SaaS service from Salesforce.com anc

delivering to and supporting the same for its business users. In the context of the event management process, the responsibility areas will be as follows:

1. XYZ, Inc. will have its end-to-end event management process for its own business application.

   a. This process will be responsible for defining a health model; developing the instrumentation the managed objects for database, middleware, application, etc.; processing events; and taking ownership of the control response on alerts and incidents at all layers above OS, including OSs that use virtual CPU, virtual memory, etc. on top of physical resources.

   b. This process will exclude the layer below the virtual machine OS running the business application.

   c. This process will still monitor the *virtual* memory, the *virtual* CPU, and the *virtual* disk and will be responsible for managing the operating system resources and taking appropriate action on alerts and incidents detected by events at the OS level.

   d. This process will monitor the availability of the virtual machine for the verification of SLA but will not own the control response for the nonavailability of the virtual machine. XYZ, Inc. would want to do this monitoring for the sake of debugging the business application (if something goes wrong, you need to check on whether a lower layer is working) and not for debugging the problem in the virtual machine.

2. Amazon, in the role of creator, will have its own event management process that will monitor all the required MOs that ensure the desired availability and performance of the virtual machine that is being delivered to XYZ, Inc. as a service. Amazon's event management process will own the responses on alerts and incidents for nonavailability and nonperformance of the virtual machine.

3. XYZ, Inc. will not require an end-to-end event management process for the Salesforce.com application, but the company will monitor the

application's availability only for the support purpose to meet its ser vice obligation toward business customers and also to measure th QoE (quality of experience) and integrations with other systems.

4. Salesforce.com, as the SaaS creator, will have its end-to-end even management process for the full stack—from physical system t applications. This will include ownership of monitoring and contrc response to meet the SLA of SaaS service for XYZ, Inc.

8 BEST PRACTICE GUIDANCE

8.1 Design Considerations

Event differentiation

When we implement tools by default, capturing and sending events is enabled for all monitors. All messages are extracted from all sources and forwarded through the event management hierarchy. This approach, while generally easy to implement, has its own merits and demerits. Events are data providers for the availability management and capacity management processes, so a good amount of data will help those processes. If you do not intend to use the data or do not have established processes for using it, then there is no point in collecting the data. On the other hand, if all captured events are not efficiently processed, then event management consoles or incident management systems, or both, will be overwhelmed with messages that may not represent actual problems. Operators and support staffs are left with the challenge of sifting through large amounts of information to determine which events or trouble tickets represent real problems and require action. Therefore the differentiation of events between actionable and nonactionable events should be done as quickly as possible and definitely within black-box processing, before they appear on the console.

Once this differentiation is established, the next level of differentiation whether the event is an alert or an incident. The purpose of this differentiatio is to apply the resources and efforts and SLA accordingly—which is primaril a commercial aspect.

Managed object database hierarchy and taxonomy

The managed object database is the foundation for the event managemer process. Historically it has been referred to as the *asset list with monitorin parameters*, but for a good process, it means much more than that. There i a lot of common data between CMDB and MO database. It is important t maintain consistency between the two to enable the sharing of data, avoi duplication, avoid inaccuracy, reduce data maintenance efforts, and improv process operations.

We know that CMDB is the center of the internal IT technology managemer universe, and its design and implementation are accorded careful consider ation. CMDB data taxonomy, such as classes, subclasses, and data element cat egorization values, are well designed. We recommend aligning the manage object taxonomy with CMDB taxonomy as much as possible and at least witl the classes and subclasses. In other words the element manager defined in th event management operation architecture should be the base class in CMDB

Even if you implement event management in isolation of CMDB, you still nee a good naming convention and taxonomy, as these are among the most impor tant standards to have. Hostnames, scripts, files, domains, and the like shoul all have consistent names across an organization because they are commonl used or referenced in automation. Depending upon the support organizatio structure, the event management process will assign or route an incident t people based on the geographic location of the failing system or on its tech nology. A standard naming convention simplifies this process, particularly ir large organizations with operations spread across many sites.

Health model

A health model is an integral part of the managed object database. It should be maintained as a part of the process management function. The primary goal of event management is to detect the deviation from normal health; therefore, the following questions become very important:

1. What is the healthy state of a managed object?

2. Can the health model change? How will the change be managed?

3. Should the system monitor for specific failure scenarios?

All these questions should be answered clearly in the health model. The health model may establish multidimensional health criteria such as availability, performance, security, and even configuration. This will help to interpret the failure scenarios related to each of these criteria. The availability and performance failure scenarios are most common and are usually the only focused criteria.

A health model documents significant information such as all actionable events, event exposure and behavior, and instrumentation protocols and behavior, and it forms the configuration datasheet for the monitoring tools. It is important to define taxonomy standards prior to documenting a health model so that the specific attribute values related to classification and prioritization levels align to a common reference.

A health model is first created at the class level that covers similar hardware and applications; an example may be a health specification for all Windows servers, and then an override is applied for a few specific deviations or subclasses—for example, a Windows server running SQL Server database.

Detection

Multiple methods can be used to detect an event of interest; these have been discussed in section 4.6.1. To determine the appropriate method, try to answer these questions: Under what conditions will the managed object events be generated? And when will the element manager need to poll the target objects?

One important rule of thumb: do not double monitor an object. By using multiple monitors to check for a single condition, you will cause processing overhead and produce redundant events that have no value. In fact, doing so will make filtering and correlation more complex and difficult.

Deliberate double monitoring is needed to validate that a problem is real and not a false positive. In this case, it is acceptable to double monitor the resource as long as the events produced by each monitor are correlated and only one is reported.

Event flow

To make the process efficient, an event-processing hierarchy should be sensibly established. In an earlier section, we noted that each event will not pass through every layer. That means you should clearly know which events are dropped at which layer and what are the value and data elements/enrichment added by each layer.

For example, if you know that an event storm is caused by the system under maintenance, then you will drop the event at the source itself. Processing is defined by the capability of tools, and you would find overwhelming options in most of the tools. But we must ask a question: do we need to do something simply because the tool provides the capability to do it?

These are the generic recommendations for efficient processing:

1. Filtering should be done at all possible stages in the processing, though it is best to filter as early as possible in the lifecycle stage. Element managers have adequate filtering capabilities.

2. Perform duplicate detection also at the element manager layer as much as possible. This saves cycles and system resources on the event

management system and saves network bandwidth used for sending unnecessary events further in the system.

3. Events can also point toward problems. Intermittent fault conditions that may clear themselves automatically and do not always require actions are actually the problems. If one of these were passed on as an incident, a support person would be frustrated to diagnose it, only to find that the incident has disappeared or requires no action. One way to handle this is to use throttling for intermittent problems that may clear themselves automatically and do not always require action. After a problem is reported, suppress or drop duplicates. For events that indicate problems always requiring action, inform when the first event is received, and suppress or drop duplicates. The incident management process should trigger the problem management process in such situations, as indicated in Figure 1.

4. It is not a good idea to create duplicate events as an escalation or reminder for an unresolved incident or warning event. The extra events create a burden not only on the system but also on the operators and assignees. The incident management process should be designed to prevent lost incidents or to track the progress of the incidents.

5. Have a comprehensive event-capture mechanism to collect the meaningful data for all processing stages and especially for correlation, but correlate only the events whose relationship is clearly understood. Sometimes you may use correlation logic that may drop genuine events because they are incorrectly deemed symptom events. It is better to have an operator manually handle these situations or something similar than to drop a genuine event.

6. Apply status-based correlation as much as possible to automatically clear problem events. This provides a better accuracy on operations— what is really in the operational pipeline.

7. Correlating events for deteriorating conditions can be tricky. While it is not feasible to create a new event for every instance of a degrading condition, it is important to ensure that appropriate escalations do take place to communicate the gravity of the issue.

8. Synchronize the status of events among event processors and the incident management system to ensure that when an event is closed or dropped at one level of the hierarchy, it is also closed or dropped at every other level. The status value of the event record is the key field for synchronization.

Event attributes

Event attributes are the fields in the event record. A typical list is given in section 4.8.1. What attributes are to be captured and what are the policies/rules for every updates are the important criteria and a matter of tool configuration. For reporting and analytics purposes, attributes should be carefully considered. Some attributes may be informational and useful only for reporting purposes, while some have an impact on the workflow and are critical for processing purposes.

Integration with incident management

Actionable events can be assigned within the event management system to the appropriate group, and their status can be tracked to their logical end. For this event management must maintain the data for assignment logic. This data can be part of the MO health model. Even though it is not necessary, it is a good idea to integrate the event and incident management processes. Integrated processes are more effective than processes working in isolation. When planning for integration, have answers ready for the following questions:

- What data is exchanged between the incident and event management processes?

- On what condition? On what trigger?

- What are the requirements for data transformation and compatibility of data between the two systems?

- Where does the responsibility of the event management system stop and that of the incident management process start?

Most of the incident management systems allow the incident to be related to a configuration item. The impacted CI information can easily come from the event management system. If a CMDB exists in the incident management system, then it is most likely to have the group data associated with the impacted CI, and the assignment logic becomes simple. Otherwise event management must supply the assignment data. There could be other data elements—such as the requestor for incident and categorization data—that are deemed mandatory in an incident management system but not in an event management system. Integration design should carefully consider how and from where to obtain those data elements—CMDB or default value?

Status synchronization between event management and incident management is critical. An event should not be closed in the incident management system but remain open in event management; this would result in the element manager in the event management process ignoring a reoccurring failure event.

Control response

When deciding on the automation of control responses on the events warranting actions, clearly define and document which events could have automated control responses and who defines these responses. This is a joint exercise between the CI/element owners and the event management implementation team, including the functional and technical consultant. Technically almost everything is possible with the addition of fancy tools. For example, you can monitor the configuration of a system in real time and, on detection of a deviation, can change the parameters on the target machine. Critical evaluation is required to examine the benefits. Very often homegrown scripts are used for several kinds of control responses and are deemed easy. But do not make these homegrown scripts a tribal knowledge in the environment. All scripts should be maintained and supported as well because they may break down at some point due to environment change and may require updates.

The following are examples of common events that are candidates for auto mated control response:

1. Restarting a service

2. Killing a process

3. Disabling access rights

4. Disabling logins

5. Submitting/restarting a batch job

6. Changing the parameter on a target machine

7. Autoscaling of cloud environments

Design for whole-service delivery

Event management should not be designed merely as the early warning system for the service health. It should go beyond that to also work as as the data provider for all other service management processes and especially for the availability man agement and capacity management processes.

Assuming that the organization has established formal processes and func tions for availability management and capacity management, it would be a joint exercise between these functional groups and the event management implementation team to obtain the data requirements and ensure that the event management process is enabled to collect the required data and is i summarised and where is it stored with easy access.

Event management is also the data provider for proactive problem manage ment. The event patterns can indicate hidden problems.

8.2 Implementation/Deployment Consideration

People and the organizational functional structure are very important for the deployment of an event management system and for ensuring that it meets its goals. The first question to ask is who are the users? This is an internal IT process: the primary users are the console operators, the secondary users are the support groups who are responsible for resolving the alerts and incidents, and the final beneficiaries are the business customers who want to be aware of the status of their services. Each of these users has his or her own requirements. Console operators want to minimize the console clutter and seek efficient filtering, while support groups also want data enrichment to enable them for quick diagnostic checks. Business customers seek a good escalation management process. They are also interested in the status awareness of the end product—the business service produced by specific business applications—and not on the underlying infrastructure. To meet the need of these different users you will require important data: the service maps.

Can you monitor each and every thing? There may be a temptation to monitor everything because tools can easily do that. However, at some point tools produces some manual work. Maintenance of process and tools is the hidden work, and we have elaborated on it in section 4.2 and section 5.1. Therefore, you should evaluate the following: How important is the service to the business? And how dependent is the business on this service? This may not be as big a problem as the demands coming from an "internal business customer." For example, an application development group may seek monitoring and control for the development server because it is important. It is a commercial decision: are you willing to spend resources on proactive support for the development environment as opposed to reactive support? A similar example is the application of a change management process that is designed to maintain the integrity of the production environment, but which some organizations choose to use for maintaining the integrity of other environments, such as the QA environment of critical business applications.

While processing the events to the closures, you will need to understand th service level requirements. This will bring up another need: establishing pr oritization/categorization and the impact/severity value matching with th CI categorization and the CI impact. You should also be aware of clusterin or mirroring configurations. A standalone server down will have differer impact than a mirrored server down or a node of a cluster down.

If you want to outsource the monitoring process, then you have to think fror the BPO outsourcing perspective. Everything should be defined in the proces to eliminate the need for tribal knowledge of your environment and the triba knowledge of your process before you can outsource. You will be responsibl to ensure that all external team members are trained in monitoring and con trol for the new services.

One very important part of the process integration is often forgotten: the chang and the release management trigger to the event management. Any environmer is never static; therefore, once the monitoring system is implemented, it needs t be configured/reconfigured according to the environment state. Release man agement will introduce new services and therefore corresponding monitore objects in the environment, but it should always be through the change man agement process, as the change management process ought to be the gatekeepe of the production environment. Execution of a change is the only event tha will trigger the adjustment in the monitoring requirements. If you monitor th environments that are not in change control, then you would design appropriat triggers to update monitoring requirements.

Likewise, the workload is not static either. Therefore you should periodicall look into the existing organizational structure and ensure that it is sufficien to handle the increased workload.

Sometimes you will be required to consider possible infrastructure constraint. that will prevent monitoring (network access, server access, user access) o some security policies that conflict with the monitoring needs. Sometimes yo may be required to work backward—that is, building the systems by design and tuning systems according to monitoring and control standards.

Governing principle for implementation

These principles are largely generic process implementation principles and written here in the context of the event management process

1. Ensure that all stakeholders agree on standards for MO and CI definition, taxonomy, KPIs, and reporting.

2. Define the MO, health model, and instrumentation during the application development lifecycle before release.

3. Define interfaces with other processes—incident, problem, change, release, availability, capacity, etc.

4. Understand the relationships between monitoring and control and other IT functions and processes.

5. Test the service several times before placing it into production to ensure that every part of the process description is in place and that the process maps correctly to the workflows.

6. Ensure that all process roles are appropriately mapped and proper training is given to the appropriate people. Document and understand all organizational dependencies.

7. Ensure that the console user sees only relevant alerts with clarity. The screen size, font size, and ambience of the monitoring workplace are very important for avoiding human error.

8. Ensure that error descriptions and troubleshooting hints are available for every alert and that all alerts are understandable, relevant, and up to date.

9. Produce meaningful reports and follow up to ensure that findings from reviews and reports actually contribute to service improvements.

8.3   Operation

The console operator team, a dedicated monitoring and control group, form a monitoring function that is commonly known as a *command center* or sometimes as an *integrated command center*. *Network operation center (NOC)* is the legacy name for the command center in which scope was limited to the enterprise network.

All monitoring should be centralized and done by the command center for the entire IT environment. All monitoring should be consolidated and correlated in the manager of managers, which will enable the command center operator to view events in a single console. If multiple monitoring tools are used, they should be integrated with or forward events to a central MoM.

The command center operators should be the owners for all events in the event management console. However, support teams may be provided access to the console to view events for the IT components they are responsible for. The command center operators should also be the owners of the defined health models and should be responsible for their maintenance, though it is the responsibility of the CI owners (e.g., server support group track leads) to provide requirements/tuning for the health models.

All events transferred as incidents to the incident management system should be automatically prioritized based on a combination of the defined health model and the CI criticality. Once qualified and forwarded events appear as the incident, the lifecycle is also controlled and managed by the incident management process.

Command center should be the owner and manager of the monitoring tool and event management processes. The command center should receive requests for monitoring or amendments to existing monitoring with a corresponding health model and data inputs in the prescribed template, and these requests must be authorized by the relevant owners. CIs that require monitoring must have appropriate instrumentation mechanisms and response rules provided by the requestor. Amendments to monitoring might be governed by change management, but amendments to the configure threshold value can be accepted by the monitoring tool administrators via a service request.

The event management tools or command center operators may directly deal with and resolve an incident (by an SOP-based control response). However, an incident ticket should be opened in the ITSM tool to maintain the consistency and integrity of the incident management process.

Suggested data retention policies for performance data from the monitoring tools are the following:

- Polling data should be held for two weeks and be summarized to one hour up to three months.

- Summarized daily data should be held for one year.

- Data older than one year should be purged.

8.4 Maturity Assessment of Event Management Process

The maturity assessment provides the basis for assessing the maturity of the event management process and establishes the foundation for tracking improvements to the process. Assessment formally collects data and analyzes it to provide an objective assessment of the maturity of the process. This is complimentary to tool portfolio optimization.

More than a decade ago, OGC published the process maturity assessment framework for ITIL service delivery and service support processes. That framework can be very effectively applied to an event management process maturity assessment. The assessment scheme under this framework is composed of an interactive interview/questionnaire that enables us to ascertain which areas are strong or weak in the overall process capability. The areas that are examined are as follows:

1. Prerequisites: Prerequisites ascertain whether the minimum level of prerequisite items are available to support the process activities.

2. Management Intent and Process Capability: Management Intent establishes whether there are organizational policy statements—that is, business objectives (or similar evidence of intent) providing both purpose and guidance in the transformation or use of the prerequisite items. This should be supported by commitment and budgets from management. Process Capability examines the activities being carried out. The questions are aimed at identifying whether a minimum set of activities is being performed.

3. Internal Integration and Products: Internal Integration seeks to ascertain whether the activities are integrated sufficiently in order to fulfil the process intent. Products examines the actual output of the process to enquire whether all the relevant products are being produced.

4. Quality Control and Management Information: Quality Control is concerned with the review and verification of the process output to ensure that it is in keeping with the quality intent. Management Information is concerned with the governance of the process and ensuring that there is adequate and timely information produced from the process in order to support necessary management decisions.

5. External Integration and Customer Interface: External Integration examines whether all the external interfaces and relationships between the discrete process and other processes have been established within the organization.

While you can hire an external consultant to deliver this assessment, you may want to perform the quick capability check of your process internally. This is amazingly simple if you follow the following steps:

1. Refer to section 4.4.1, which lists the outputs that should be delivered by the process. Use this as a checklist.

2. Verify whether those outputs are generated.

    a. If yes, examine the quality of output and identify quality gaps.

        i. From the quality gaps, determine the correct level of output and go to the next step.

    b. If no, then ask the question, Is the required input available to produce that output?

        i. If yes, then there is some process activity gap that can be easily identified by using the process diagrams of section 4.2.

        ii. If no, then list this as the input gap.

3. Refer to the process diagrams in section 4.2 and make an activity checklist. Verify whether these activities are performed in the tools or outside the tools and whether there is any missing activity.

This is the simplest approach, and it is highly productive in finding the gaps and the clues for remediation as well.

9 SECURITY MANAGEMENT FOUNDATION

Hitherto we have been talking about event management as the founda tion of IT operations management, but it is a strong foundation fo security management as well. In a way, it is a specialized implementatio of the event management process with some additional features and func tionality. The common event management process should be extended acros the security-monitoring environment, and we can even extend the sam manager of managers to provide a common event process. However, becaus the function that consumes these alerts also performs the security-specifi control actions that might be governed by risk and compliance guideline we recommend that the function performing security monitoring should b kept exclusive. Some of the additional standards are developed for securit event management, such as Cisco SDEE (Security Device Event Exchange and IETF's IDMEF (Intrusion Detection Message Exchange Format). Man more investments are being made in event management for security monitor ing than those that are being made for operations management. The Nationa Institute of Standards and Technology (NIST) has taken an important ini tiative in this area around EMAP and SCAP (Security Content Automatio Protocol). There are multiple and interrelated development initiatives towar standardizations, and we want to highlight the specifics around EMAP as i relates to the event management process.

9.1 EMAP: Event Management Automation Protocol

The primary goal of the Event Management Automation Protocol (EMAP) is to expand the effectiveness of the NIST Security Automation Program by establishing a suite of specifications standardizing the communication of digital event data. EMAP will be a peer of SCAP.

Another goal of the EMAP program is to develop and implement an EMAP Validation Program that will ensure compliance with EMAP specifications and increase the effectiveness of procurement decisions within organizations.

EMAP is attempting to standardize the machine communications within the event management domain, while SCAP is focused on configuration, vulnerability, and asset management. EMAP notionally includes the following components, and, though they are connected with the EMAP program, each one of them is a separate initiative:

1. Common Event Expression (CEE): A suite of specifications to define taxonomy, syntax, transport, logging recommendations, and parsing information about event records

2. Open Event Expression Language (OEEL): A language to express parsing and normalization logic using CEE profiles to convert event records into CEE

3. Common Event Rule Expression (CERE): A common format to express rules for pattern matching, filtering, and correlation

4. Common Event Scoring System (CESS): A specification that provides metrics of event severity and impact based on multiple factors

5. Cyber Observable eXpression (CybOX): A language to express cyberobservable events or stateful measures that provides a common foundation for many of the other standards

Effective analysis of an event record requires parsing and comprehension. Parsing events is hard, and comprehending events is harder. CEE solution includes standardization of CEE Log Transport (CLT), CEE Log Syntax (CLS) and CEE Dictionary and Event Taxonomy (CDET) to figure out what "type" of event it is and what the event means.

The second problem to address is to enable EMAP parsing logic authoring and parsing logic migration and sharing activities. This will enable third-party tools to transform proprietary log data into a standardized event data model. The plan is to develop OEEL (Open Event Expression Language)—standardized expression language for log transformation logic to support decouple translation of proprietary log data to a standardized format.

Through OEEL, NIST is aiming to standardize the data exchange, not the implementation. Since data exchange happens at the interfaces between systems, the OEEL data models will ensure consistent semantics across system boundaries will be more expressive. It is expected that proprietary tools will optimize these exchange models for execution.

The next problem to address is to enable EMAP rule authoring, rule migration, and sharing activities. This will be addressed by Common Event Rule Expression (CERE), which will provide vendors and consumers a way to express and share rules for correlation, filtering, and aggregation of event data. CERE will use existing event data vocabularies to enable the assertion of specific relationships when certain data patterns exist (e.g., an incident is occurring if the following events are seen) and it will not be executable, as it is only meant for translation into executable languages.

Event management in the cybersecurity domain is a specialized domain by itself, and it has brought in some new definitions—namely, cyber observable and CybOX. A cyber observable is a measurable event or stateful property in the cyber domain, and CybOX (Cyber Observable eXpression) is a standardized language for encoding and communicating high-fidelity information about cyber observables, whether dynamic events or stateful measures are observable in the operational cyber domain.

CybOX is not targeted at a single cybersecurity use case but rather is intended to be flexible enough to offer a common solution for all cybersecurity use cases requiring the ability to deal with cyber observables. By specifying a common structured schematic mechanism for these cyber observables, the intent is to enable the potential for detailed automatable sharing, mapping, detection, and analysis heuristics of cybersecurity events.

10 INDUSTRY SCENARIOS: AUTHORS' VIEWS

The business of IT needs is going through a fundamental shift in terms of how IT is being fused with the business, and in some cases the business itself. IT has always been focused on automating the business via systems and processes, but when it comes to IT's own processes and systems, it has been like the cobbler's son who doesn't have good shoes to wear. All businesses have strong business processes and they first make strong processes and then automate it through IT Systems, but IT people are generally least focused on business processes for their business.

Instead, a unified approach to managing the evolution of the landscape is needed. The big disruptions, like IOT, SMAC, big data and legacy to cloud, are leading to the evolution of a "digital enterprise business" where the consumption models are also changing, which is in turn leading to a need for a common IT operating model that can handle the fluid state.

The BSM Architecture of the future provides a reference point and guidance for creating a platform to achieve this vision. The BSM Architecture is divided into three layers—namely, Managed Entities, Platform Services, and Business Services—that connect the providers and consumers using unified architecture. There are a total of thirty-five subdomain areas, which comprise multiple capabilities across the entire stack. (See the Appendix for the definitions of these subdomains.)

If we are to enable this vision, it needs to be simplified into the interactions that happen across the entire IT service value chain. The entire IT value chain can be classified into the following cornerstones:

1. People
2. Process
3. Devices/Machines
4. Data

Each of these layers is interconnected with the others, and a synchronization of the value chain leads to the following flows:

1. H2H (Human to Human)—People interact and collaborate with people in delivering IT services, which leads to a connection between people and processes that in turn generates transactions classified as *human-to-human transactions.*

2. H2M (Human to Machines)—People interact with devices/machines/ applications from an operational perspective to perform changes/con- figurations as simple or complex task actions, which leads to *human- to-machine transactions.*

3. M2M (Machine to Machine)—Applications/systems/devices interact and generate lots of machine data across the *machine-to-machine com- munications.* The type of data generated is vast, semistructured, and high velocity.

4. IP (Intelligent Processing)—The data generated by machines, when connected to the process, generates *intelligent processing insights,* which lead to *operational intelligence.*

The future of event management systems will evolve into the fulcrum for deliv- ering operational intelligence, which will enable IT to provide insights that allow the digital business to take decisions/control actions in real time. The key aspects to look out for these new systems are the following capabilities:

1. Real-time monitoring, including streaming feeds
2. Unified collection layer across IT operations/digital ops and security ops

3. Real-time situation detection and diagnostics
4. Real-time role specific and domain-specific visualization
5. Application topology intelligence across hybrid environments (on-premises/hosted/cloud)
6. Correlation across events and data feeds with anomaly detection and pattern detection
7. OMDB to be based on big-data store
8. Multidimensional predictive analytics
9. Search-driven diagnostics
10. Automated resolution via self-learning/knowledge-driven engine

11 APPENDIX

Domains and Subdomains in BSM Architecture

Domain	Subdomain	Function Area	Repository
Managed Entities	Platform Management	Event detection	Multiple Native Repositories
		Config tracking	
		Performance monitoring	
		Job scheduling	
		Security administration	
		Network management	
		Systems management	
		Application management	
	Cross-Platform Management	Workload automation	Multiple Native Repositories
		Data management	
		Code management	
		Provisioning	
		Discovery	
		Usage tracking	
		Deployment management	
		Transaction monitoring	
		Log management	
		Change tracking	
		Facilities management	
		Console consolidation	

Platform Services	**Collect & Transform**	Event consolidation	Multiple Native Repositories
		Task consolidation	
		Identity consolidation	
		Discovery	
	Orchestration & Policy Automation	Correlation engine	OMDB based on Big Data Store
		Topology intelligence	
		Diagnostics	
		Predictive analytics	
Business Services	**IT Service Management**	16 process areas	10 datastores (including Asset DB & CMDB)
	Business Service Management	8 process areas	2 datastores
	Management Information Presentation	Self-service	1 datastore
		Service analytics	1 datastore
		Dashboard	1 datastore

ABOUT THE AUTHORS

Prafull Verma

Prafull Verma has a bachelor's degree in electronics and communication engineering and has over thirty years' experience in the area of electronic data processing and information technology. He started his career in India in the area of electronic data processing systems and later moved to the United States in 1997. During the past thirty years, he has worked on diversified areas in computer science and information technologies. Some of his key experience areas are the design and implementation of heterogeneous networks, midrange technical support management, end-user service management and design, and the implementation and management of process-driven ITSM systems.

Prafull has acquired a unique blend of expertise in integrated areas of tools, process, governance, operations, and technology. He is the author of several methodology and frameworks for IT service management that include multivendor ITIL frameworks, ITSM for cloud computing and Service Integration.

Prafull's competencies and specializations include the area of merging engineering with service management, as this book manifests, and outsourcing business management.

Currently, Prafull is working for HCL Technologies Ltd., Infrastructure Service Division, and Cross Functional Service Business Unit, as chief solution architect. He is also serving member of the product advisory council of Service Now, the industry leading ITSM platform.

Kalyan Kumar

Kalyan Kumar (KK) is the Chief Technologist for HCL Technologies – ISD and leads all the Global Technology Practices.

In his current role Kalyan is responsible defining Architecture & Technology Strategy, New Solutions Development & Engineering across all Enterprise Infrastructure, Business Productivity, Unified Communication Collaboration & Enterprise Platform/DevOps Service Lines. Kalyan is also responsible for usiness and Service Delivery for Cross Functional Services for HCL across all rvice lines globally.

alyan is widely acknowledged as an expert and path-breaker on BSM/ITSM IT Architecture and Cloud Platforms and has developed many IPs for the mpany in these domains. He is also credited with building HCL MTaaS™ rvice from the scratch, which has a multi-million turnover today and a pro-rietary benchmark for Global IT Infrastructure Services Delivery. His team also credited with developing the MyCloud™ platform for Cloud Service Management & MyDevOps, which is a pioneering breakthrough in the Utility omputing and Hybrid Agile Ops Model space. He has been presented with any internal and industry awards for his thought leadership in the IT Management space.

alyan also runs the HCL ISD IPDEV Incubator Group where he is responsi-le for incubating new services, platforms and IPs for the company. He is also ctive in the Digital Systems Integration Roadmap and Solutions Strategy for CL. He has also co-authored a Book **"Process Excellence for IT Operations: practical guide to IT Service Management" (http://tinyurl.com/k7u3wyf)** nd two more books are in pipeline of being published

alyan has spoken at many prestigious industry platforms and is currently actively ngaged in Partner Advisory Board of CA Technologies, IBM Software etc.

1 his free time Kalyan likes to jam with his band Contraband as a drummer / ercussionist and reviews Consumer Technology Gadgets and follows Cricket ames Diligently. Kalyan lives in New Delhi, India with his family.

K can be followed on Twitter @KKLIVE and at Linkedin (http://www.linkedin. om/in/kalyankumar).

FROM THE SAME AUTHORS

Process Excellence for IT Operations

PROCESS EXCELLENCE
FOR IT OPERATIONS

While everyone is talking about the ITIL framework, this book is touching process engineering, design, and maintenance and support topics- the subject hitherto unaddressed by any other publication.

As the title suggests, the book is providing a practical guidance on managing the processes for IT Services. There are lot of guidance available on technology management in IT industry but this book is focusing on technology independent service management. The book will be addressed to all IT people from a process practitioner perspective, however, the fundamentals are presented in simplistic terms, and therefore it should be useful to all IT people. It will describe the process engineering concept and how it can be applied to IT Service Management. This is not about the industry standard framework such as ITIL and COBIT but about the common processes that are generally used in real life operations. I will be using analogies and illustrations from non-IT world also to make the things simple. This book does not focus on any technology.

What are the readers' comments about this book on Amazon?

5.0 out of 5 stars

Awesome Read, January 8, 2014

This is one of its kinds and superb read. I highly recommend to IT business profe sionals and anyone who wants to adapt processes at work place and in personal lif

5.0 out of 5 stars

Best book for IT Consultants, May 1, 2014

This is one of the unique book that I have ever seen which gives the complete sigl which ITIL does not gives. This book has all the information from the practicali point of implementing IT Process and make it process driven operations rather ju. implementing the processes in IT environment. The writer has written every b of information where an IT operations can be improved using the guidelines pre vided in this book. One book to have for Process Design, Process Implementatior Process Maturity and Process improvement is Process excellence for operations

5.0 out of 5 stars

Great book for IT Professionals, April 30, 2014

Sincere efforts were made with clear concepts for IT professionals to understar the practicality in managing the process for IT services. I like the Technology independent approach of the writers; all the books that I have come across unt now are more technology dependent. Process engineering concepts and the sim plistic approach of the writers has made me come to the conclusion that thi book is like a Bible for all IT professional

FROM THE SAME AUTHORS

Service Integration – The cornerstone of Service Management

Service Integration

Prakash Verma and Kalyan Kumar

Trends are changing in Corporate Services also. The technology exposure of an individual is not just in the premise of their office. In fact now a days the computing environment in individual's home is much more modern that the computing environment that corporation provides in the workplace. Users are demanding more and more when they see the availability of personal IT services in external world- Dropbox and App Stores for example. The only way for corporation to meet the demand is to pool in more and more service providers and integrates their services. Eventually corporations' mainstream function will be service integration and operation integration.

In recent past the term **SIAM** (Service Integration And Management) is gaining popularity in corporate IT world. This is popularized by British Government's Service Design manual that defines **SIAM** as following -

"Service Integration And Management lets an organization manage the service providers in a consistent and efficient way, making sure that performance across a portfolio of multi-sourced goods and services meets user needs."

Made in the USA
San Bernardino, CA
24 August 2014